Programmed Learning Aid for

INTERMEDIATE ACCOUNTING

Volume 2

Programmed Learning Aid for

INTERMEDIATE ACCOUNTING

VOLUME 2

GLENN A. WELSCH, Ph.D.
The John Arch White Professor of Accounting
The University of Texas at Austin
and Certified Public Accountant (CPA)

WALTER T. HARRISON, JR., Ph.D.
Assistant Professor of Accounting
The University of Texas at Austin
and Certified Public Accountant (CPA)

Coordinating Editor
ROGER H. HERMANSON
Georgia State University

LEARNING SYSTEMS COMPANY

A division of
RICHARD D. IRWIN, INC. Homewood, Illinois 60430

Also available through
IRWIN-DORSEY LIMITED Georgetown, Ontario L7G 4B3

ISBN 0-256-01988-6
Printed in the United States of America

1 2 3 4 5 6 7 8 9 0 K 6 5 4 3 2 1 0 9 8 7

FOREWORD

Each of the books constituting the Programmed Learning Aid Series is in programmed learning format to provide the reader with a quick, efficient, and effective means of grasping the essential subject matter.

The specific benefits of the programmed method of presentation are as follows:

1. It keeps the reader *active* in the learning process and increases comprehension level.
2. Incorrect responses are *corrected immediately*.
3. Correct responses are *reinforced immediately*.
4. The method is *flexible*. Those who need more "tutoring" receive it, because they are encouraged to reread frames in which they have missed any of the questions asked.
5. The method makes learning seem like a game.

The method of programming used in this PLAID on intermediate accounting and in most of the other PLAIDS is unique and simple to use. Begin by reading Frame 1^1 in Chapter 1. At the end of that frame answer the True-False questions given. To determine the correctness of your responses, merely turn the page and examine the answers given in Answer frame 1^1. You are told *why* each statement is true or false. Performance on the questions given is used as a measure of your understanding of all the materials in Frame 1^1. If any of the questions are missed, reread Frame 1^1 before continuing on to Frame 2^1. This same procedure should be used throughout the book. Specific instructions are given throughout as to where to turn next to continue working the program.

You may desire to go through the PLAID a second time leaving out the programmed questions and answers, or to test your understanding by going through it a second time, answering all of the questions once again and rereading only those frames in which comprehension is unsatisfactory.

PLAIDS are continuously updated in new printings to provide readers with the latest subject content in the field.

Dr. Welsch, coauthor of the PLAID for intermediate accounting, is also a coauthor of a leading text in intermediate accounting and has taught the subject matter for many years. Dr. Harrison is extensively engaged in teaching and research in financial accounting.

The user will find the coverage to be "student oriented" in that the essential subject matter is presented in a concise, uncomplicated, and effective manner.

Roger H. Hermanson
Coordinating Editor

PREFACE

This Programmed Learning Aid was written in response to a need by several groups for a concise and especially designed source of review materials covering the subject matter. The two volumes comprising the PLAID for intermediate accounting are not designed to be used as a textbook in the subject but rather as supplements to any standard work. They are especially appropriate for study and review purposes on a self-study basis where time constraints are critical; thus, they are recommended especially for the following groups: college students enrolled in an intermediate accounting course, students starting a master's degree program in business administration, participants in executive development programs, individuals in business, and any other individual wishing to review the subject matter of intermediate accounting.

The subject matter is organized in a sequence that follows logically and in the order that is generally followed in most of the well-known intermediate accounting texts. Atlhough the material generally should be approached sequentially by the beginner, those who are actively enrolled in a related course or are reviewing will find that the chapters can be studied on a selective basis since each one represents a complete unit. Each chapter has been developed so as to focus on and explain concisely the *significant* concepts and procedures so that the reader is not immersed in a bulk of detail.

The special features of this PLAID have been designed in response to the stated objective, that is, to provide a concise, organized, and effective plan of study and review of the subject matter for the reader. To this end the PLAID incorporates the following special features:

1. Concise and direct explanations in each chapter of the fundamental concepts and procedures.
2. Short and to-the-point illustrations that utilize simple figures to enhance the understanding of basic concepts and procedures.
3. Careful identification of subject matter with appropriate captions and subcaptions.
4. Short chapters that can be reviewed in 40 to 55 minutes.
5. Programming of questions and answers for review so that the reader can evaluate his progress in the subject matter while he is reading each chapter. Several sets of programmed questions and answers will be found in each chapter.
6. A total of six examinations in the two volumes designed specifically to duplicate the *types* of questions utilized in most intermediate accounting courses. These examinations are classified by subject matter (chapters); they are challenging and thought provoking. The answers are provided; therefore, this aspect of the PLAID should be especially attractive to those readers who use it concurrently with registration in intermediate accounting.

7. Underscoring or italicizing of important distinctions and key words (phrases) in order to direct attention to specific points that may be overlooked by the reader.
8. In each volume a complete table of contents and an index to facilitate the location of specific subjects included in the PLAID.

Experience has suggested that utilization of a well-designed learning aid as a supplement to a textbook tends to increase the student's demonstrated grasp of the subject matter with a minimum of additional effort. Also it is a handy reference for refreshing one's memory on a specific topic or group of topics.

The authors welcome suggestions and constructive comments in respect to the materials and presentations included in this PLAID.

GLENN A. WELSCH
WALTER T. HARRISON, JR.

CONTENTS

Volume 2

Volume 1

chapter 15

CORPORATIONS—FORMATION AND CONTRIBUTED CAPITAL

Frame 1[15]

Nature of Corporations

The laws of each state provide for the formation and operation of corporations. These laws differ from state to state; however, there is much similarity in basic provisions. Of particular importance is the fact that all states provide for the existence of a corporation as a *separate entity;* that is, legally, a corporation is viewed as being separate and apart from its shareholders. To form a corporation, all states require that an application for a *charter* be submitted by the organizers. Upon approval of the application by the state a charter is issued. The charter specifies such items as the type of business that may be conducted, the types and amounts of authorized stock, and the methods of electing officers. Corporations typically are classified as:

1. Public corporations, when they relate to governmental units or business operations owned by governmental units.
2. Private corporations, when they are privately owned. Such corporations may be nonstock (nonprofit organizations such as colleges and churches) or stock (usually a business organized for profit making).
3. Domestic corporations, when operating in the state in which incorporated.
4. Foreign corporations, when operating in states other than the one in which incorporated.
5. Open corporations, when the stock is available for purchase. The stock is usually widely held.
6. Closely held corporations, when the stock is not available for purchase and is generally held by a few shareholders.

Concept of Corporate Capital

In accounting for a corporation, unique problems are encountered primarily with respect to capital (owners' equity). Two distinct equities are recognized: (1) creditors' equity, consisting of all corporate liabilities; and (2) owners' equity, consisting of capital contributed by the owners, retained earnings, and unrealized capital. In accounting for corporate proprietary equities, accountants follow the overriding concept that *sources of capital must be separately recorded and reported.* To apply this concept, numerous corporate capital accounts are established and reported on the balance sheet and statement of retained earnings. In accounting for corporations, capital sources must be identified in order that *legal* or *stated* capital can be determined and considered in making sound and legal decisions. Legal capital is that portion of corporate capital that is required by statute to be permanently retained in the business for the protection of creditors. In most states legal capital is represented by the *par value* of all shares of stock outstanding, and in the case of nopar-value stock, by either a stated value per share outstanding or, in the case of true nopar stock, the total amount paid in to the corporation upon initial sale of the stock.

Nature of Capital Stock

Ownership in a corporation is represented by stock certificates. Shares may be transferred at will by the owner thereof. This is one of the major advantages of the corporate form of business. Each share of stock carries the following basic rights (unless withheld by the charter and specified on the stock certificates):

1. The right to participate in the *management* of the corporation through participating and voting in stockholder meetings.
2. The right to participate in the *profits* of the corporation through dividends declared by the board of directors.
3. The right to share in the distribution of *assets* of the corporation at liquidation or through "capital" dividends.
4. The right to purchase shares of stock on a *pro rata basis* in the corporation when such shares represent additional capital stock issues. This right is designed to protect the proportional interest of each shareholder in the ownership. In recent years, this *preemptive* right has increasingly been specifically withheld.

These rights are shared equitably and proportionately (based on the number of shares owned) by all shareholders; however, the charter may withhold rights from one class of stock and not from another.

Corporate Capital

In order to understand the accounting for corporate capital, the following terms must be clearly understood.

1. Authorized capital stock—the number of shares of stock that can be issued legally as specified in the charter.
2. Issued capital stock—the number of shares of authorized stock that have been issued to date.
3. Unissued capital stock—the number of shares of authorized capital stock that have *never* been issued.
4. Outstanding capital stock—the number of shares of stock that have been issued and are being held by shareholders at a given date.
5. Treasury stock—those shares once issued and later reacquired by the corporation.
6. Subscribed stock—unissued shares of stock set aside to meet subscription contracts. Subscribed stock will be issued upon full payment of the subscription price or as otherwise specified in the subscription contract.

In the accounting for and the reporting of corporate capital by *sources,* the following balance sheet categories have evolved, although there are some variations in terminology to be found in practice:

1. Contributed capital (sometimes referred to as paid-in capital):
   a. Capital stock.
      (1) Preferred stock.
      (2) Common stock.

b. Other contributed capital:
   (1) From owners—amounts paid in excess of par or stated value (often called premium on stock).
   (2) From outsiders—donations of assets.
2. Retained earnings:
   a. Appropriated (also referred to as reserves).
   b. Unappropriated.
3. Unrealized increment (unrealized gain) or decrement (unrealized loss).

In reporting corporate capital on the balance sheet, emphasis should be on the *source of capital* and clarity of presentation. The *capital section* of a balance sheet is shown in Illustration 15–1, which illustrates the above categories and preferred terminology.

Illustration 15–1
Stockholders' Equity

Contributed Capital:			
Capital stock:			
Preferred stock, 6% par $10, cumulative and nonparticipating, 20,000 shares authorized, 15,000 issued		$150,000	
Preferred stock subscribed, 100 shares		1,000	
Total		151,000	
Common stock, nopar value, authorized 10,000 shares, issued and outstanding 8,000 shares at stated value, $5 .		40,000	$191,000
Other Contributed Capital:			
By owners:			
From sale of preferred stock in excess of par value . .		12,000	
From sale of common stock in excess of stated value .		3,000	15,000
By outsiders:			
From donation of plant site			5,000
Total Contributed Capital			211,000
Retained Earnings:			
Appropriated:			
For bond sinking fund	$40,000		
For possible loss on lawsuit pending	10,000	50,000	
Unappropriated		70,000	
Total Retained Earnings			120,000
Unrealized loss on long-term investments			(50,000)
Total Stockholders' Equity			$281,000

Indicate whether each of the following statements is true or false by writing *T* or *F* in the space provided.

______ 1. Private corporations refer to those corporations which are held by only a few shareholders and the stock of which is not publicly traded.

______ 2. Unless specifically withheld in the contract under which stock is sold by the corporation, all four basic rights attach to ownership of the shares.

______ 3. Contributed capital is equal to the par value of stock in most cases.

______ 4. The balance in the capital stock accounts is determined by multiplying the number of shares issued by the par value of each share.

______ 5. Unrealized capital (increments as well as decrements) is an element of retained earnings.

Now check your responses by comparing them with Answer Frame 1[15], page 4.

Answer frame 1[15]

1. False. Private corporations are owned by groups other than government. The description given in the question refers to closely held corporations.
2. True. However, it is fairly common, for example, for preferred stockholders to be specifically precluded in the stock contract from voting.
3. False. Contributed capital is in fact determined by shareholders' contributions to the corporation. In most cases this does not equal par value. There is no necessary relationship between par value and any other element of stockholders' equity.
4. True. A common misunderstanding is that the balance in the stock accounts is equal to par value per share multiplied by the number of shares outstanding. This latter case is true only when there are no treasury shares held by the corporation.
5. False. The facts that (*a*) this layer of capital is specifically entitled "unrealized" and (*b*) it is listed separately on page 3 are evidence that it is not an element of retained earnings.

If you missed any of the above questions, reread Frame 1[15] before proceeding. Then, turn to Frame 2[15], below, and continue reading.

Frame 2[15]

Classes of Capital Stock

Typical corporate structures utilize a number of different classes and types of capital stock, subject to certain restrictions imposed by the laws of the state of incorporation. The two primary classifications of capital stock are (*a*) par-value and nopar-value stock, and (*b*) common and preferred stock. Each of these classications is reviewed below.

Par-Value Stock. Par-value stock has a designated "value" per share as specified in the charter of the corporation as approved by the state of incorporation. This value must be printed on the face of each stock certificate. Par-value stock may be either common or preferred stock. Since the owners of a corporation have limited liability (that is, generally they are not liable beyond the assets of the corporation), the laws of most states provide that the par value is to provide a measure of protection to the creditors. Stock initially sold for less than par by the issuing corporation is said to be sold at a *discount;* this is illegal in most states. Stock sold for an amount in excess of par is often said to be sold at a *premium.* In recent years, despite illegality, shares have been sold at an actual discount in cases where assets other than cash were used to purchase the shares and those assets were overvalued to avoid recording the discount. In accounting for par-value stock the capital account is credited for the par value of the shares issued (sold) and any excess is credited to a contributed capital account such as Contributed Capital in Excess of Par Value.

Nopar-Value Stock. True nopar stock does not carry a designated or assigned "value" per share, nor is such provided for in the charter. Nopar-value stock may be either common or preferred stock. The primary advantages of nopar stock are that (*a*) it avoids the possibility of having to record a discount on issuance, (*b*) it does not mislead the investor into believing that par value has some relationship to market value, (*c*) it facilitates accounting for corporate capital, and (*d*) it does away with the expediency of overvaluing noncash assets that are exchanged for shares. In recent years, the practice of issuing nopar stock with an *assigned* or *stated* value has grown. This type of stock is a hybrid between par and true nopar-value stock; it is accounted for in the same manner as par-value stock. In accounting for true nopar-value stock, as a general principle, the total amount received from the initial sale is credited to the capital stock account.

Common Stock. Common stock represents the basic issue of stock of the corporation and normally carries all of the rights listed on page 2. Where a corporation has one class of stock, it must be common stock. All other classes of stock, that is, those with *special* provisions, are customarily referred to as preferred stock.

Preferred Stock. Stock having a special priority (which may be positive, such as a dividend preference, or negative, such as nonvoting) is known as preferred stock. The preference may be related to one or more of the following:

1. Preferred as to *dividends:*
   a. Cumulative or noncumulative.
   b. Fully participating, partially participating, nonparticipating.
2. Preferred as to *assets.*
3. Preferred as to *redemption.*
4. Preferred as to *convertibility.*

In the absence of stipulations to the contrary, preferred shares carry all of the basic rights listed earlier such as the right to vote. Preferred stock usually is par value, and dividend preference is stated as a percentage of par value. For example, 6% preferred stock would carry a dividend preference of 6% of the par value of each share. In the case of nopar preferred stock, the dividend preference would be stated at a specific dollar amount per share.

Cumulative Dividend Preferences. Noncumulative preferred stock provides that dividends not declared (passed) for any particular year or series of years are lost permanently as far as the preferred shareholder is concerned. Alternatively, cumulative preferred stock provides that dividends passed (dividends in arrears) for any year or series of years must be paid to the preferred shareholders *prior* to the payment of dividends to common shareholders. If only a part of the preference for any year is not paid, the unpaid part carries over as dividends in arrears. The stock certificates must state the nature of this and any other preferences.

Participating Dividend Preferences. Preferred stock is fully participating when the preferred shareholders are entitled to extra dividends (above the basic preference) on a pro rata basis (based on par or stated values) with the common shareholders. In this case the preference provides a *prior* claim only up to the preferential rate. Preferred stock that is nonparticipating limits the amount of dividends payable to the preferred shareholders to the preferential rate specified in the charter and on the stock certificate. Partially participating preferred stock provides for a prior claim each year up to the preferential rate, then an additional stated participation rate which applies as a participation with the common shareholders. For example, a corporation may issue 6% preferred stock, with participation limited to an additional 2%; in this case participation privileges with the common shareholders would be limited to a total of 8% of par value of the preferred stock.

Other Preferences. Stock preferred as to *assets* provides that upon dissolution the holders thereof will have first priority for return of liquidated assets up to the par value of the stock held (or a stated amount above par); the remainder of the assets would then be distributed to the common shareholders. Stock preferred as to *redemption* provides that under specified conditions each preferred shareholder has the option to turn in shares owned for reimbursement at a specified price per share. Stock preferred as to *convertibility* provides that the preferred shareholder has the option to turn in shares owned and receive in return specified shares (e.g., common shares) in a stipulated ratio.

Computation of Dividends. Accountants are frequently called upon to aid management in the computation of dividends. In order to illustrate dividend computations, the following example and solutions under several assumptions are provided.

Assumed data as to stock outstanding:

Preferred stock, 5% ($100 par value per share—1,000 shares) . . .	$100,000
Common stock ($100 par value per share—2,000 shares)	200,000

Solution for four different situations:

	Preferred	*Common*
Illustration No. 1: Preferred stock is cumulative, nonparticipating; dividends two years in arrears; dividends declared, $28,000.		
Step 1—Preferred in arrears	$10,000	
Step 2—Preferred, current (at 5%)	5,000	
Step 3—Common (balance)		$13,000
	$15,000	$13,000
Illustration No. 2: Preferred stock is cumulative, fully participating; dividends two years in arrears; dividends declared, $28,000.		
Step 1—Preferred in arrears	$10,000	
Step 2—Preferred, current (at 5%)	5,000	
Step 3—Common, current (to match preferred at 5%)		$10,000
Step 4—Balance (ratably with par)	1,000	2,000
	$16,000	$12,000
Illustration No. 3: Preferred stock is noncumulative, partially participating up to 7%; dividends declared, $28,000.		
Step 1—Preferred, current (at 5%)	$ 5,000	
Step 2—Common, current (to match preferred at 5%)		$10,000
Step 3—Preferred, partial participation, additional 2%	2,000	
Step 4—Common (balance)		11,000
	$ 7,000	$21,000
Illustration No. 4: Preferred stock is noncumulative; partially participating up to 7%; dividends declared, $16,000.		
Step 1—Preferred, current at 5%	$ 5,000	
Step 2—Common, current (to match preferred at 5%)		$10,000
Step 3—{ Preferred, partial participation	333	
Step 3—{ Common		667
	$ 5,333	$10,667

Determine whether each of the following four statements is true or false. Then work Problem 5.

______ 1. The issuance of capital stock at a discount is legal in most states.

______ 2. Nopar-value stock with a stated value is recorded in the same manner as par-value stock.

______ 3. The dividend preference on nopar preferred stock is stated at a specific percentage of current market value.

______ 4. Convertible preferred stock is convertible at the option of the corporation and not at the option of the shareholder.

______ 5. Refer to the capital structure used above to illustrate the computation of dividends. Preferred stock is cumulative and fully participating up to 7%. Dividends are one year in arrears. What is the minimum total amount of dividends which will provide $14,000 total dividends for common stockholders?

Now check your responses by comparing them with Answer Frame 2[15], page 8.

Frame 3[15]

Legal Capital

Legal capital, sometimes referred to as stated capital, is defined by state law. Legal capital is a part of the total owners' equity and in many cases is less than the amount paid in by shareholders. Since the laws of the various states define legal capital somewhat differently, we must generalize. Generally speaking, legal capital is defined as the par value (par-value stock), the stated or assigned value (nopar stock), or the total amount paid in the case of *true* nopar-value stock. Legal capital is the primary basis for accounting and reporting for corporate capital by *source*. The amount of legal capital, as defined by law, should be entered in the *Capital Stock account;* and *any* contributed capital in excess of par or stated value should be entered in other appropriately designated capital accounts.

Accounting for Par-Value Stock

Since accounting by *source* is necessary, account titles such as Common Stock; Capital Stock, 5% Preferred; and Common Stock-Nopar, should be used in recording the legal capital. Any excess amount paid in (above legal capital) requires the use of appropriately named accounts, such as Contributed Capital in Excess of Par Value of Common Stock. The normal sequence of transactions relating to the issuance of stock is (*a*) authorization of the shares, (*b*) receipt of subscriptions, (*c*) collections on subscriptions, and (*d*) issuance of the shares. In order to review this sequence of entries for *par-value stock,* the following situation is presented, with appropriate journal entries and comments:

Authorization: Blue Corporation was authorized in its charter to issue 5,000 shares of common stock, par value $100 per share.

Entry: Memorandum only, as follows:

Capital stock, common—par value $100 per share; authorized 5,000 shares. (Enter in journal and in heading of the ledger account, Common Stock.)

(Note: Alternatively, a formal journal entry could be made debiting Unissued Common Stock and crediting Authorized Common Stock for $500,000.)

Subscriptions: Blue Corporation received subscriptions from interested parties for 3,000 shares of the common stock at $110 per share.

Entry:

Stock subscriptions receivable—common stock	330,000	
Common stock subscribed (3,000 shares)		300,000
Contributed capital in excess of par, common		30,000

Collections on subscriptions: Blue Corporation, in accordance with the contract, collected 40 percent of the subscription price from each subscriber.

Entry:

Cash ($330,000 × 40%)	132,000	
Stock subscriptions receivable—common stock		132,000

(Note: Normally no shares are issued to a shareholder until his or her shares are paid for in full.)

Issuance of shares: Blue Corporation collected the remainder from each subscriber and issued the shares.

Entry:

Cash ($330,000 − $132,000)	198,000	
Stock subscriptions receivable—common stock		198,000
Common stock subscribed (3,000 shares)	300,000	
Common stock (3,000 shares)		300,000

Answer frame 2[15]

1. False. In most states the sale of capital stock at a discount is illegal.
2. True. Nopar-value stock with a stated value is recorded in the same manner as par-value stock; the stated value is handled as if it were par value.
3. False. The dividend preferences on nopar preferred stock is stated at a specific dollar amount per share.
4. False. Convertible preferred stock is convertible at the option of the shareholder only.
5. $26,000. Computations:

	Preferred		*Common*		
Preferred dividends, in arrears, one year	$ 5,000				
Preferred dividends, current year	5,000				
Common dividends, current year			$10,000		
Participation, on the basis of relative par values	2,000		4,000		
Totals	$12,000	+	$14,000	=	$26,000

Notice that in addition to the preferred dividends in arrears, preferred shareholders receive a maximum of $7,000 dividends in any one year.

If you missed any of the above questions, reread Frame 2[15] before proceeding. Then turn to Frame 3[15], page 7, and continue reading.

Frame 3[15] continued

Accounting for Nopar-Value Stock

Nopar stock having an *assigned* or *stated* value is accounted for exactly as illustrated above for par-value stock; the assigned or stated value is treated as if it were par value. The illustration below is presented to review accounting for *true* nopar-value stock.

Authorization: Red Corporation was authorized in its charter to issue 10,000 shares of nopar-value common stock.

Entry: Memorandum only, as follows:

Common stock, nopar-value; authorized 10,000 shares.

Subscriptions: Red Corporation received subscriptions to 6,000 shares for $245,000.

Entry:

	Debit	Credit
Stock subscriptions receivable—common stock	245,000	
Common stock subscribed, nopar (6,000 shares)		245,000

(Observe that there is no premium or discount to be recorded on true nopar-value stock; the entire amount received should be recorded in the *legal* capital account.)

Collections on subscriptions: Red Corporation collected, per the agreement, one half of the subscription price from each subscriber.

Entry:

	Debit	Credit
Cash	122,500	
Stock subscriptions receivable—nopar common stock		122,500

(Note: Normally no shares are issued to a shareholder until his or her shares are paid for in full.)

Issuance of shares: Red Corporation collected the balance due from each subscriber and issued the shares.

Entry:

	Debit	Credit
Cash ($245,000 − $122,500)	122,500	
Stock subscriptions receivable—nopar common stock		122,500
Common stock subscribed, nopar (6,000 shares)	245,000	
Common stock, nopar value (6,000 shares)		245,000

In accounting for true nopar-value stock, it is especially important that the number of shares involved be recorded in each entry, since there is no common "conversion factor" such as the par or assigned value per share.

Defaults on Stock Subscriptions

Occasionally a subscriber to stock in a corporation fails to make complete payment in accordance with the subscription contract; however, in the usual case at least a down payment will have been made when the contract was signed. In such cases the corporation, in the absence of a legal requirement, may elect either to (*a*) return all cash received from the subscriber and cancel the subscription contract or (*b*) issue all shares equivalent to the cash received from the subscriber to date. To illustrate, assume a subscription contract for $10,000 par-value stock priced at $10,500 with a down payment of $4,200; this transaction would be recorded as follows:

Cash	4,200	
Stock subscriptions receivable—capital stock	6,300	
Capital stock subscribed		10,000
Contributed capital in excess of par		500

Now assume the subscriber defaults and the corporation decides to return the cash and cancel the subscription contract; the prior entry must be completely reversed:

Capital stock subscribed	10,000	
Contributed capital in excess of par	500	
Stock subscriptions receivable—capital stock		6,300
Cash		4,200

Instead, now assume that when the subscriber defaults the corporation decides to issue stock equivalent to the cash paid; in this case 40 percent of the shares subscribed must be issued (that is, $4,200 ÷ $10,500 = 40%). The entry is:

Capital stock subscribed	10,000	
Contributed capital in excess of par ($500 × 60%)	300	
Stock subscriptions receivable—capital stock		6,300
Capital stock ($10,000 × 40%)		4,000

The laws of some states have specific provisions as to what must be done in case of default. One provision requires forfeiture of the stock; but the corporation must resell the stock under a lien whereby there must be a refund to the original subscriber for cash paid, less additional cost of reselling. The maximum amount to be paid the defaulting subscriber is the total of the cash payments to date of default. In this case a *payable to subscriber* must be recorded pending resale, at which time a settlement is effected with the original subscriber. To illustrate, utilizing the above data:

Entry to record the default and to establish a payable:

Capital stock subscribed	10,000	
Contributed capital in excess of par	500	
Stock subscriptions receivable—capital stock		6,300
Payable to subscriber (name—pending resale)		4,200

Entry to record resale at $11,000 and a $600 cost of resale:

Cash ($11,000 − $600)	10,400	
Payable to subscriber (original sale $10,500—resale $10,400)	100	
Capital stock		10,000
Contributed capital in excess of par (original amount protected)		500

Entry to record final settlement with the original subscriber:

Payable to subscriber (account balance)	4,100	
Cash		4,100

Accounting for Stock Premium and Discount

Additional contributed capital (premium on stock) identified with the class of stock to which it pertains should be reported on the balance sheet as a subcategory of contributed capital with a general designation such as "other contributed capital" (see illustration on page 3). Discount should be reported under this same subcategory and should be reported as a separate item and not offset against premium as a net amount.

True or false?

______ 1. Contributed capital in excess of par should not be recognized on stock subscriptions until the subscriptions are fully paid.

______ 2. Premium on issue of stock has the s[illegible]ne effect on the balance sheet as net income.

______ 3. Accounting for corporate capi[illegible] (or owners' equity) by source has its basis in the legal capital r[illegible]rement.

______ 4. The most that a subsc[illegible] who defaults on his or her stock subscription can expect [illegible]ceive from the corporation is the amount paid in prior to default.

Now check your responses by comparing them with Answer Frame 3[15], page 12.

Frame 4[15]

Special Sales of Stock

In some cases corporations issue stock in blocks comprised of different classes of stock (e.g., preferred and common). The apportionment of the stockholders' equities created by such a sale of stock should be made on the basis of relative current market values of the two classes of stock. Alternatively, if a current market value is determinable for only one class of stock, the market value of that class is subtracted from the issue price of the entire block and the remaining equity is credited to the other class of stock. If the current market values are not determinable for either class of stock, the equities may be apportioned on the basis of relative par values.

To illustrate apportionment on the basis of relative current market values, assume that a corporation issues 100 shares of common stock (par value $100) along with 50 shares of preferred stock (par value $80) in exchange for cash of $15,000. At the issue date the common is widely quoted at $104 and the preferred at $101.

Entry:

Cash	15,000	
Preferred stock		4,000
Contributed capital in excess of par, preferred		903
Common stock		10,000
Contributed capital in excess of par, common		97

Computations:

Preferred: $\frac{\$5,050}{\$15,450} \times \$15,000 = \$4,903 - \$4,000 = \$903$

Common: $\frac{\$10,400}{\$15,450} \times \$15,000 = \$10,097 - \$10,000 = \$97$

Noncash Sales of Stock

When a corporation issues stock in exchange for services or assets other than cash, the valuation of the assets or services received (or alternatively, the sales price of the stock) presents a problem. The values to apply, in order of preference, are:

1. Current market value of assets or services received.
2. Current market value of stock issued.
3. Current appraisal value of assets or services received.
4. Current valuation or assets or services established by the board of directors.

Incorporation of a Going Business

The owner, or owners, of a proprietorship or partnership may decide to incorporate the business. Normally, the proprietor, or the partners will receive stock of the newly formed corporation in exchange for some or all of the net assets of the proprietorship or partnership. In effect, there is a purchase transaction. Therefore, the owners of the predecessor entity will demand corporation stock with a value equal to the fair market value of the net assets (assets less liabilities) given up. Any excess of fair value of stock issued over the fair market value of specifically identified net assets received by the corporation is recorded as purchased goodwill by the corporation.

To illustrate, assume that XY Corporation issues 1,000 shares of common stock (par value $5) with a current fair market value of $10 in exchange for the net assets of X and Y Partnership. X and Y shared partnership profits in a 3 to 1 ratio. At the date of incorporation, the X and Y Partnership balance sheet appears thus:

Cash	$ 800	Current liabilities	$ 1,000
Accounts receivable	2,000	Bonds payable	3,000
Inventories	5,000	X, capital	6,000
Fixed assets	7,000	Y, capital	2,800
Accumulated depreciation	(2,000)		
	$12,800		$12,800

At the time of the exchange, the inventories of the partnership had a fair market value of $4,500 and the fixed assets (with a book value of $5,000) had a current fair market value of $6,000. Assume that the partnership books are to be retained.

Given the above facts, the entries to record the incorporation would be:

1. To adjust the assets to fair market value:

Fixed assets	1,000	
Inventories		500
Adjustment account		500

2. To recognize goodwill:

Goodwill*	700	
Adjustment account		700

*Computations:

Value of stock as given (1,000 shares at $10)	$10,000
Value of net assets, after adjustment ($8,800 + $500)	9,300
Goodwill	$ 700

3. To close Adjustment Account to partners' capital accounts (apportioned in partnership profit ratio):

Adjustment account ($500 + $700)	1,200	
X, capital (¾ × $1,200)		900
Y, capital (¼ × $1,200)		300

4. To record distribution of stock to the partners, and to close the partners' capital accounts:

X, capital ($6,000 + $900)	6,900	
Y, capital ($2,800 + $300)	3,100	
Common stock (1,000 shares at $5)		5,000
Contributed capital in excess of par, common		5,000

Answer frame 3[15]

1. False. At the point at which the corporation receives the subscription, it has an enforceable claim against the subscriber. This claim is in fact a receivable, which conforms to the definition of an asset. Therefore, the transaction also creates an equity in the entire amount of the subscription (which in most cases will include a premium of subscription price over par).
2. False. Premium on an issue of stock (i.e., contributed capital in excess of par) is an element of contributed capital. Net income becomes part of retained earnings, another separate element of stockholders' equity. Thus, the two elements, premium on stock and net income, both reflect increments to assets and stockholders' equity. However, they arise from different sources and as such affect the balance sheet differently.
3. True. Most states have legal capital requirements designed to protect creditors' claims against corporations. This requirement dictates the need to account for corporate capital by source.
4. True. In some states, the amount of refund is fixed by statute. Generally, the burden rests with the defaulting subscriber to perform on his or her contract. In some states, however, the corporation has considerable latitude in the amount of the refund, if any, to make to the defaulting subscriber.

If you missed any of the above questions, reread Frame 3[15] before proceeding. Then turn to Frame 4[15], page 10, and continue reading.

Frame 4[15] continued

After incorporation, the XY Corporation balance sheet would appear as follows:

Cash	$ 800	Current liabilities	$ 1,000
Accounts receivable	2,000	Bonds payable	3,000
Inventories	4,500	Common stock	5,000
Fixed assets	8,000	Contributed capital in excess of par	5,000
Accumulated depreciation	(2,000)		
Goodwill	700		
	$14,000		$14,000

True or false?

_______ 1. When two or more classes of stock are sold jointly at a single price, the equities should be apportioned to the two classes of stock on the basis of relative par values.

_______ 2. Corporation A issues 1,000 shares of its common stock to acquire a building that is reflected on the seller's books at $25,000. The seller estimates that the building is worth $55,000. Corporation A's stock is quoted on the American Stock Exchange at a market value of $52.50 on the day of the exchange. Corporation A should record the building at a cost of $52,500.

_______ 3. From a theoretical standpoint, the assets and liabilities of a partnership (or proprietorship) which the owners formally incorporate should be revalued to current market values because the corporation in effect purchases the net assets of the partnership (or proprietorship).

_______ 4. Net asset revaluations pursuant to incorporation of a partnership should be closed to the partners' capital accounts and apportioned thereto on the basis of relative partners' capital balances.

Now check your progress against the answers given at Answer Frame 4[15], page 14.

chapter 16

CORPORATIONS—RETAINED EARNINGS AND DIVIDENDS

Frame 1[16]

The Concept of Retained Earnings

There are three major categories of corporate capital: contributed capital, retained earnings, and unrealized capital increment (or decrement). This chapter reviews retained earnings. Retained earnings represent the *accumulated* earnings and losses of a corporation reduced by (1) dividend distributions to shareholders and (2) any amount transferred to contributed capital (such as through a stock dividend). Earnings and losses may have come from regular operations and extraordinary items. Reductions may also have come from capital stock transactions.

Total retained earnings are represented by two groups of accounts: *unappropriated* retained earnings (generally recorded in the single account Retained Earnings) and *appropriated* retained eranings (usually recorded in several accounts, as indicated later in the chapter). Retained earnings must be labeled in such a way that the *source* is identified and reported. "Retained earnings" is the preferred terminology.

It is reemphasized that in accounting for retained earnings, as with respect to other elements of corporate capital, reporting in terms of *source* is of fundamental importance in order to facilitate compliance with legal requirements involving capital.

The primary *reductions* of retained earnings are occasioned by (1) cash dividends, (2) stock dividends, (3) treasury stock requirements (see Chapter 17), (4) recapitalizations (see subsequent section of this chapter), and (5) absorption of losses.

Nature of Dividends

Dividends are distributions by the corporation to shareholders in proportion to the number of shares owned; such distributions tend to be at regular intervals (such as quarterly). Dividends of the following types are encountered with some frequency:

a. Cash dividends (distribution of corporate cash).
b. Property dividends (paid with assets other than cash).
c. Liability or scrip dividends (cash dividends with an extended payment date).
d. Liquidating dividends (a return of shareholder capital).
e. Stock dividends (not a distribution of assets).

Answer frame 4[15]

1. False. The classes of stock should be apportioned on the basis of relative market values because the proceeds from the sale of the stock represent the market values of stock, not the par value. However, where no market values are available or reliable, relative par values may be used.
2. True. In general, assets are valued at cost, which means the cash price of what is *given* for the assets. In this case no cash is given for the building. But 1,000 shares of stock, with a cash price of $52.50 per share, are given. Therefore the cost of the building is $52,500. Another important factor in this problem is the fact that the *value* of the stock appears to be more objectively determinable than the value of the building.
3. True. The corporation pays for the net assets (i.e., assets less liabilities, or stockholders' equity) at current market value, not at book value which might have arisen at some distant earlier time and which might differ greatly from current value.
4. False. The apportionment should be made on the basis of the profit and loss sharing ratio because net asset revaluations represent gain or loss to the partners. Relative partners' capital balances are used as a basis for apportioning asset distributions in liquidation because the capital accounts represent owners' equities in the entity's assets.

If you missed any of the above, restudy Frame 4[15] before turning to Chapter 16, page 13.

Frame 1[16] continued

Generally speaking, the distribution of a dividend requires *both* assets (cash) and retained earnings; thus the entry for a $10,000 cash dividend would be:

Retained earnings (unappropriated)	10,000	
Cash		10,000

The laws of all states allow unappropriated retained earnings to be used for dividend purposes; there are legal constraints in some states, such as restrictions with respect to the cost of treasury stock held. Under specified conditions, some states permit debits to particular contributed capital accounts (such as Contributed Capital in Excess of Par) as a basis for stock dividends, and even for cash dividends if creditor interests are not jeopardized. However, in the absence of specific information to the contrary it should always be presumed that the debit for dividends will be to *Unappropriated* Retained Earnings.

Accounting for dividends involves three important dates:

1. Date of declaration. This is the date that the board of directors of the corporation formally announces a dividend declaration. If a *nonrevocable* dividend (cash, property, or liability dividend) is involved, the corporation incurs a liability and therefore must make an entry for the dividend declaration on this date, viz:

Retained earnings	10,000	
Cash dividends payable		10,000

   A stock dividend is revocable; hence no entry need be made on this date.
2. Date of record. This is the date selected by the board of directors (and stated in the formal dividend announcement) on which the list of shareholders to receive the dividend is to be prepared from the corporate records (shareholders' subsidiary ledger). *No accounting entry is made on this date.*
3. Date of payment. This is the date selected by the board of directors (and stated in the formal dividend announcement) on which payment is to be made. The corporation must make a formal accounting entry on this date, viz:

Cash dividends payable	10,000	
Cash		10,000

In the case of a *stock dividend* the distribution is recorded on this date as illustrated later in the chapter.

Cash Dividends. The usual form of distribution to shareholders is a cash dividend. The declaration of a dividend must meet all preference requirements of preferred stock and then may extend to common stockholders. (See Chapter 15 for computation of dividends.) The balances of Cash and Unappropriated Retained Earnings are important considerations in the declaration of a cash dividend. A cash dividend declaration and payment was illustrated in the preceding paragraph. Any balance in the Cash Dividends Payable account should be reported on the balance sheet as a current liability.

Property Dividends. Dividends paid in assets other than cash are known as property dividends. The accounting is the same as for a cash dividend; however, it is necessary first to revalue the dividend property at its *current* fair market value. The theory underlying the revaluation is that in this nonreciprocal disposal of assets, the laws of supply and demand do not impact on the market value of the dividend property. As a result, shareholders receive the fair market value of the property as though they were receiving the cash equivalent. Gain or loss on disposal of the asset is recognized in the revaluation. Then the dividend payment entry is recorded at the current market value (which then equals book value) of the property to be distributed to shareholders.

Liability Dividends. Strictly speaking, any dividend between declaration date and payment date is a liability dividend; however, the term is used to indicate those instances where the board of directors has announced an extended period of time (such as one, two, or three years) between these two dates. Such declarations are occasioned by shortages in cash. In such cases a formal document "scrip" generally is sent to the shareholders, and it may or may not be interest bearing. Liability dividends are recorded in the same manner as cash dividends; during the period between declaration and payment dates the balance in the Liability Dividends Payable account should be reported on the balance sheet as current or noncurrent, depending upon the time element involved.

Liquidating Dividends. Distributions that constitute a *return of capital* rather than a disbursement of assets from earnings are known as liquidating dividends; such distributions may be intentional or unintentional. They are intentional when the board of directors knowingly declares a return of capital, as in the case when the corporation is contracting capital or gradually liquidating. *Shareholders must be notified formally when a liquidating dividend is involved* because a liquidating dividend is not taxable income to the shareholder. Rather, it serves to reduce the cost basis of his or her stock. Unintentional liquidating dividends occur when net income (hence retained earnings) is overstated and a dividend is declared in an amount that dips into the overstated portion of retained earnings. In accounting for liquidating dividends, contributed capital accounts (rather than retained earnings) are debited; in some cases a special account such as Capital Repayment may have to be debited. The balance in such an account would be reported as a deduction in the contributed capital section of the balance sheet.

Indicate whether each of the following statements is true or false by writing *T* or *F* in the space provided.

______ 1. Retained earnings (including appropriations) is one of the three major categories of corporate contributed capital.

______ 2. A corporation with three shareholders transferred corporate title to certain real estate to its shareholders in proportion to shares which they held; this was a property dividend.

______ 3. Appropriations of retained earnings temporarily reduce total retained earnings pending removal of the appropriation.

______ 4. In a sense, the term "liquidating dividend" is a misnomer because a return of capital does not conform to the definition of a dividend.

Now check your responses by comparing them with Answer Frame 1[16], page 16.

Answer frame 1[16]

1. False. Retained earnings, contributed capital, and unrealized capital are the three major categories of *corporate* capital. Therefore, retained earnings is a *separate* section of capital *from* contributed capital.
2. True. This was a *property dividend* since it was paid in assets other than cash.
3. False. Appropriated retained earnings is a part of total retained earnings. It is just not a part of unappropriated retained earnings.
4. False. See the definition of dividends given on page 13. But because some would define dividends as solely distributions of profits, the answer could also be "true" if one adopts this alternative definition.

If you missed any of the above questions, reread Frame 1[16] before proceeding. Then turn to page 2[16], below, and continue reading.

Frame 2[16]

Stock Dividends

A stock dividend is a distribution of additional shares of stock to the shareholders in proportion to the current holdings. It may involve the distribution of either treasury stock or unissued stock. A stock dividend does not involve the disbursement of *corporate assets,* such as cash or other assets. There are three primary reasons why stock dividends are utilized by corporations:

1. To convert retained earnings balances into *permanent* capital.
2. To continue some form of dividends to shareholders without utilizing cash or other assets.
3. To increase the number of shares outstanding, thus reducing the market price per share (to hopefully encourage trading of shares in the market).

Since a stock dividend involves the *transfer* of some amount from retained earnings to the contributed capital accounts, the question arises as to how much should be transferred in a given situation. State laws and accounting principles have tended to establish a minimum and a maximum amount, viz:

1. Minimum—the par, stated, or assigned value; or in the case of true nopar-value stock, the average amount per share originally paid in.
2. Maximum—the fair market value (at the date of declaration) of the *additional* shares issued.

The general guidelines in determining the amount of retained earnings that should be capitalized are:

a. A small stock dividend—if the proportion of additional shares being issued as a stock dividend is small (20 percent has been used as the guideline) in proportion to total shares outstanding the *maximum* (fair market value) *should be capitalized.*

b. A large stock dividend—if the proportion is large (over 20%) the *minimum* (par value) should be capitalized.

c. Managerial discretion may elect the average amount originally paid in as a better choice under the existing conditions.

In order to illustrate the three situations involving stock dividends, assume the following data:

Preferred stock, par value $20, 10,000 shares authorized, 5,000 shares issued and outstanding	$100,000	
Common stock, par value $10, 20,000 shares authorized, 10,000 shares issued and outstanding	100,000	
Contributed capital in excess of par, preferred	10,000	
Contributed capital in excess of par, common	15,000	
Retained earnings	150,000	
Total Stockholders' Equity		$375,000
Market price per share:		
Preferred	$ 25	
Common	11	

Situation 1—A small stock dividend; capitalize the maximum (fair market value). A 10% stock dividend was declared on the common stock; the market price per share did not change perceptibly. The entry at date of issuance:

Retained earnings (1,000 shares × \$11)	11,000	
Common stock (1,000 shares × par \$10)		10,000
Contributed capital in excess of par, common (1,000 shares × \$1)		1,000

Note that no entry is needed on the date of declaration of a stock dividend. This is due primarily to the fact that subsequent to declaration, the corporation may legally revoke the declaration. Also, note that the stock dividend entry involves no liability (which it does in the case of a cash dividend) because the stock dividend makes no claim on the assets of the corporation. Stock dividends thus involve only an intra-equity shift from Retained Earnings to Capital Stock (i.e., Contributed Capital).

Situation 2—A large stock dividend; capitalize the minimum (par value). A 50% common stock dividend was declared on the common stock; the market price dropped perceptibly, to \$7.50 per share. The entry at date of issuance:

Retained earnings (5,000 shares at par \$10)	50,000	
Common stock (5,000 shares)		50,000

Situation 3—The management decided to capitalize the average amount per share *paid in*. A 50% common stock dividend was declared on the common stock; the market price dropped to \$7.50 per share. The entry at date of issuance to capitalize average paid in:

Retained earnings (5,000 shares × \$11.50*)	57,500	
Common stock (5,000 shares at par \$10)		50,000
Contributed capital in excess of par, common		7,500

* Computation: (\$100,000 + \$15,000) ÷ 10,000 shares = \$11.50

Reporting Unissued Stock Dividends on the Balance Sheet

If a balance sheet is prepared between declaration date and payment (issuance) date, the fact that a stock dividend has been declared is generally disclosed in a footnote.

Stock Split

A *true* stock split should be differentiated from a stock dividend. In the case of a stock dividend (as reviewed above) an amount of *retained earnings* is *transferred to permanent (legal) capital*. In contrast, in a true stock split there is no such transfer. In a *true stock split* the number of shares outstanding is increased by reducing proportionately the par value *per share;* thus a stock split does not affect retained earnings nor *total permanent (legal) capital*. The significant difference between a stock dividend and a stock split is that only the former *increases permanent* capital; *total* capital is not changed by either. To illustrate, assume X Corporation has 10,000 shares of \$10 par value common stock outstanding and retained earnings of \$175,000; that is, a total capital of \$275,000. The following tabulation compares the effects of two means of effecting a 100% increase in outstanding shares (i.e., a 100 percent stock dividend and a 2 for 1 stock split):

	Balances after Change	
	Stock Dividend	*Stock Split*
Capital Stock:		
Number of shares	20,000	20,000
Par value	× \$10	× \$5
Total	\$200,000	\$100,000
Retained earnings	75,000	175,000
Total Capital after Change . . .	\$275,000	\$275,000

A true stock split requires only a memorandum entry in the accounts to reflect the lower par value per share and the increased number of shares outstanding.

Determine whether each of the three following statements is true or false.

______ 1. For a stock dividend, there will be a transfer of retained earnings to contributed capital.

______ 2. For a stock dividend, the amount of retained earnings to be capitalized will depend on whether the dividend is small or large relative to shares outstanding.

______ 3. Stock dividends that are declared but not yet issued should be reported as current liabilities.

Solve the following problem involving a stock dividend.

______ 4. Corporation X, whose $40 par-value common stock is currently selling at $50 per share, has decided to issue a stock dividend. Authorization is for 200,000 shares, with 100,000 issued and outstanding. The corporation desires to capitalize $400,000 of the retained earnings balance. Compute the stock dividend percentage that will accomplish this objective.

Now check your responses by comparing them with Answer Frame 2[16], page 20.

Frame 3[16]

Appropriations of Retained Earnings

From time to time it may be desirable to set aside retained earnings in the accounts and on the financial statements; such an *appropriation* of retained earnings constitutes a *restriction* on a specified portion of retained earnings. It must be remembered, however, that appropriations still represent a part of the *total* retained earnings, and when the need for the appropriation ceases to exist the appropriated amount should be returned to unappropriated retained earnings. The credit balance in appropriated retained earnings accounts should never be utilized to absorb losses or other charges (debits); thus an appropriated retained earnings account should *never be debited* except to return the balance (or a part of the balance) to the unappropriated retained earnings account.

There are four primary reasons why retained earnings may be appropriated; they are:

1. To fulfill a *legal requirement,* as in the case of a legal restriction on retained earnings equal to the cost of treasury stock owned (see Chapter 17).
2. To fulfill a *contractual agreement,* as in the case where a bond issue requires a restriction on retained earnings as a protection for the bondholders.
3. To record formally a *discretionary management decision* to restrict retained earnings *as a matter of financial planning;* appropriation withholds the specified amount from dividends. An example of this situation would be the establishment of an account such as Retained Earnings Appropriated for Future Expansion.
4. To record formally a *discretionary management decision* to restrict a portion of retained earnings *in anticipation of a possible future loss,* such as Retained Earnings Appropriated for Future Casualty Losses. It should be emphasized, as noted above, that this account would *not* be used to absorb such losses should they actually occur; the only purpose in making the appropriation is to restrict the amount of dividend declarations.

Some examples of the points outlined immediately above are illustrated in the following situations.

Situation 1—To fulfill a legal requirement. The XY Corporation purchased 1,000 shares of its own stock in the open market at $20 per share; state laws require that dividends be restricted to the amount of retained earnings in excess of the cost of treasury stock. The indicated entries would be:

a. To record purchase of the treasury stock (cost method):

Treasury stock (1,000 shares common stock)	20,000	
Cash		20,000

b. To record the appropriation (restriction) of retained earnings:

Retained earnings	20,000	
Retained earnings appropriated for the cost of treasury stock held		20,000

c. To record sale of one half of the treasury stock at $20 per share:

Cash	10,000	
Treasury stock (500 shares)		10,000

d. To record removal of the related appropriation:

Retained earnings appropriated for the cost of treasury stock held	10,000	
Retained earnings		10,000

Situation 2—To fulfill a contractual agreement. The AB Corporation issued $50,000 bonds payable at par; the bond indenture provided that retained earnings equal to the bonds outstanding would be restricted from dividends.

a. To record sale of the bonds and to appropriate retained earnings:

Cash	50,000	
Bonds payable		50,000
Retained earnings	50,000	
Retained earnings appropriated for bonds outstanding		50,000

Concurrent with this appropriation, the corporation may also establish a bond sinking fund (of assets) in the amount of $50,000. In the absence of a contractual agreement to this effect, however, there is no requirement that the fund be established.

At the date that the bonds are retired the above entries would be reversed.

Situation 3—To record a discretionary management decision. The management, in recognition of the fact that considerable funds (earnings) had been invested in fixed plant, decided to appropriate retained earnings approximately equivalent to the $200,000 thus invested.

a. To record the appropriation:

Retained earnings	200,000	
Retained earnings appropriated for investment in fixed assets		200,000

b. Normally, appropriations of this type remain in the accounts indefinitely; however, the management may later decide to "capitalize" the amount of earnings through a stock dividend. Let's assume this decision has been made; the entries would be:

To return the appropriation:

Retained earnings appropriated for investment in fixed assets	200,000	
Retained earnings		200,000

To record the stock dividend:

Retained earnings	200,000	
Capital stock		200,000

Answer frame 2[16]

1. True. Stock dividends always require the capitalization of *some* amount of retained earnings.
2. True. For small stock dividends, the fair market value should be capitalized; for larger stock dividends, as a minimum the par or stated value should be capitalized. Fair market value is generally greater than par value.
3. False. Stock dividends prior to issue are reported by footnote. They do not affect liabilities because they make no claim on assets (recall the definition of a liability).
4. Eight percent. Computations:

$400,000 ÷ Par value or current market value per share = Number of dividend shares.

Try par value of $40:

$400,000 ÷ $40 = 10,000 shares ÷ 100,000 shares outstanding = 10%, is a "small" stock dividend, which should be recorded at fair market value. Thus, try market value:

$400,000 ÷ $50 = 8,000 shares ÷ 100,000 shares outstanding = 8%.

If you missed any of the above questions, reread Frame 2[16] before proceeding. Then turn to Frame 3[16], page 18, and continue reading.

Frame 3[16] continued

Indicate whether each of the following statements is true or false by writing *T* or *F* in the space provided.

______ 1. When retained earnings are appropriated, this has the effect of placing a restriction on specified assets of the corporation.

______ 2. Appropriations of retained earnings can be used to avoid reporting of major losses on the income statement.

______ 3. The total amount of retained earnings is temporarily reduced when a reserve for bond sinking fund is established.

______ 4. The creation of a bond sinking fund causes a decrease in Retained Earnings.

Now check your responses by comparing them with Answer Frame 3[16], page 22.

Frame 4[16]

Reporting Retained Earnings

Extraordinary gains (losses) and prior period adjustments have traditionally been associated with the Retained Earnings account. The association of the former category is an indirect one, whereas the latter association is direct. That is, extraordinary gain and losses are elements of net income (like revenues and expenses). Thus, like all other *income statement accounts,* extraordinary gains and losses are closed into the Retained Earnings account in the end-of-period closing process.

Prior period adjustments, on the other hand, represent items of gain or loss that should have been reflected on the income statement of a prior accounting period. However, because they were not known (or an error was made), such items are not detected until a later accounting period. Thus, the accountant must record the item as a prior period adjustment which is later closed directly to the Retained Earnings account. This effectively bypasses the income statement entirely. Prior period adjustments, rather than outright accounting errors, are rare.

1. Extraordinary items should be reported on the income statement in the following manner:

Income before extraordinary items . . .		$XXX
Extraordinary items (gains and losses) . .	$XXX	
Less: Applicable income tax	XXX	XXX
Net Income		$XXX

   Extraordinary items are defined as events and transactions that are distinguished by their unusual nature *and* by the infrequency of their occurrence. Thus, *both* of the following criteria must be met to classify an item as extraordinary: (a) Unusual nature—the underlying event or transaction must be of a type that is clearly unrelated to, or only incidentally related to, the ordinary and typical activities of the entity, taking into account the environment in which the entity operates; (b) Infrequency of occurrence—the underlying event or transaction must be of a type that would not reasonably be expected to occur again in the forseeable future, taking into account the environment in which the entity operates.
2. Prior period adjustments should be reported on the statement of retained earnings; they are defined as those *material* adjustments which to be so classified must meet *all* of the following four criteria: (*a*) can be specifically identified with and directly related to the business activities of particular prior periods, (*b*) are not attributable to economic events occurring subsequent to the date of the financial statements for the prior period, (*c*) depend primarily on determinations by persons other than management, and (*d*) were not susceptible of reasonable estimation prior to such determination. Examples are: adjustments of income taxes and litigation claims that arose in an earlier accounting period.

The following income statement and statement of retained earnings illustrate correct presentation of both *extraordinary items* (on the income statement) and *prior period adjustments* (on the statement of retained earnings).

MODEL STORES, INCORPORATED

Income Statement
For the Year Ended December 31, 1977

Sales		$520,000
Less: Cost of goods sold		300,000
Gross margin		220,000
Less: Operating expenses	$120,000	
Income taxes	52,000	172,000
Income before extraordinary items		48,000
Extraordinary items:		
Loss of plant due to earthquake	10,000	
Less: Applicable tax saving	6,000	4,000
Net Income		$ 44,000

Answer frame 3[16]

1. False. When retained earnings are appropriated, there is no restriction on specific assets. Appropriations of retained earnings do not relate to any identifiable assets. Until unappropriated, there is a restriction on the amount of dividends that can be paid.
2. False. All losses (except prior period adjustments) must be reported on the income statement. Appropriations of retained earnings cannot be charged for losses of any type.
3. False. A reserve for bond sinking fund is an appropriation of retained earnings. Appropriations of retained earnings are part of total retained earnings; therefore, total retained earnings is not reduced when such a reserve is established.
4. False. The creation of a bond sinking fund causes a decrease in cash.

If you missed any of the above questions, reread Frame 3[16] before proceeding. Then turn to Frame 4[16], page 20, and continue reading.

Frame 4[16] continued

MODEL STORES, INCORPORATED

Statement of Retained Earnings
For the Year Ended December 31, 1977

Unappropriated Retained Earnings:				
Unappropriated balance, January 1, 1977			$120,000	
Adjustments applicable to prior periods:				
Refund from renegotiation of 1975 income taxes		$27,000		
Damages from lawsuit (1976)	$15,000			
Less: Tax saving	7,000	8,000	19,000	
Corrected balance			139,000	
Add: Net income for current year			44,000	
			183,000	
Deductions and appropriations:				
Dividends		30,000		
Appropriation for bond sinking fund		10,000	40,000	
Unappropriated balance, December 31, 1977				$143,000
Appropriated Retained Earnings:				
Reserve for bond sinking fund, balance January 1, 1977		40,000		
Addition for current year		10,000		
Reserve for bond sinking fund, balance December 31, 1977			50,000	
Appropriation for plant expansion			60,000	
Appropriated balance, December 31, 1977				110,000
Total Appropriated and Unappropriated, Balance, December 31, 1977				$253,000

Quasi-Reorganizations

A quasi-reorganization is a procedure whereby a corporation having major financial difficulties can establish a new basis for accounting for assets and corporate capital without formal court proceedings. A quasi-reorganization is appropriate when a corporation has sustained heavy losses to the point where insolvency is a real possibility. Frequently, such situations are characterized by an overstatement of assets and corporate capital (there may also be a significant deficit in retained earnings). The quasi-reorganization procedure has been sanctioned by the accounting profession (and the Securities and Exchange Commission) under certain conditions and safeguards which are listed below:

1. Upon completion of the quasi-reorganization, retained earnings must be zero.
2. The effect of the procedure must be reported in full to all shareholders.
3. Upon completion of the quasi-reorganization no capital account shall show a deficit.
4. A fair and conservative balance sheet must be presented immediately after completion of the quasi-reorganization in order to obviate as far as possible future reorganizations of a like nature.

The primary characteristics of a quasi-reorganization are:

a. Appropriate asset accounts are written down.
b. The capital accounts are restated.
c. The Retained Earnings account (adjusted to a zero balance) must be "dated" for a reasonable period of time (usually five to ten years) following the reorganization. This disclosure alerts users of the financial statements to the fact that the Retained Earnings account does not reflect the entire earnings history of the corporation.
d. The corporate entity is unchanged.

To illustrate, assume the following balance sheet prior to quasi-reorganization:

Current assets . . .	$100,000	Capital stock . . .	$750,000
		Premium on stock . .	50,000
Fixed assets	500,000	Retained earnings . .	(200,000)
	$600,000		$600,000

Included in the current assets are inventories that are clearly overvalued by $25,000; in the fixed asset total it appears that there are assets overvalued by $125,000.

The management considered recommending two alternatives to the shareholders: (1) liquidate the corporation and (2) effect a quasi-reorganization. The shareholders agreed to the second alternative and the following entries were made:

a. To write down the assets to a realistic value:

Clearance account—quasi-reorganization	150,000	
Current assets (inventories)		25,000
Fixed assets (specific accounts)		125,000

b To eliminate the deficit in retained earnings:

Clearance account—quasi-reorganization	200,000	
Retained earnings		200,000

c. To write off the stock premium account:

Premium on stock	50,000	
Clearance account—quasi-reorganization		50,000

d. To close the clearance account and hence reduce legal capital from $750,000 to the new net value of $450,000:

Capital stock	300,000	
Clearance account—quasi-reorganization		300,000

The balance sheet after the quasi-reorganization would appear as follows:

Current assets . . .	$ 75,000	Capital stock	$450,000
Fixed assets	375,000	Retained earnings (dated)	—
	$450,000		$450,000

True or false?

_______ 1. Extraordinary items are identified solely by their infrequency of occurrence.

_______ 2. Extraordinary gains are reported on the income statement, whereas extraordinary losses are reported on the statement of retained earnings.

_______ 3. Prior period adjustments are reported on the income statement of the period to which they apply.

_______ 4. Retained earnings are always eliminated in the case of a quasi-reorganization.

Now check your responses by comparing them with Answer Frame 4[16], page 26.

chapter 17

CORPORATIONS—CONTRACTION AND EXPANSION OF CORPORATE CAPITAL AFTER FORMATION; AND EARNINGS PER SHARE

Frame 1[17]

Changes in Capital after Formation

Subsequent to formation, a corporation may change its capital structure by (*a*) selling new issues of stock, (*b*) changing par values of current issues, (*c*) calling in outstanding shares (callable shares), (*d*) converting one class of stock into another class, or (*e*) purchasing its own shares to be held for future resale (treasury stock) or to be canceled. In accounting for such changes three basic principles have general applicability:

1. Accounting must be such that *sources* of all capital are recorded and reported accurately in order to facilitate compliance with legal requirements as to the classes of stock that may be used to declare dividends.
2. Since a corporation cannot realize income on capital transactions between itself and its owners, ac-

counting recognition of increases in net assets resulting from transactions relating to the corporation's own stock involve additions to *contributed capital* rather than to retained earnings.

3. Certain payments by a corporation to its shareholders for their shares above the original contributions may be considered to be a form of cash dividends (thus affecting retained earnings).

Treasury Stock

The laws of most states permit a corporation to purchase shares of its own stock subject to certain limitations. *Treasury stock* may be defined as a corporation's own stock that (*a*) has been issued, (*b*) has been subsequently reacquired by the issuing corporation, and (*c*) has not been resold or canceled. Treasury stock when resold once again is classified as outstanding stock. The purchase of treasury stock serves to *reduce* both the corporation's assets and its capital; alternatively, the resale of treasury stock serves to *increase* both assets and capital. There are two generally recognized and mutually exclusive concepts underlying accounting for treasury stock transactions: the "one-transaction" concept and the "dual-transaction" concept. Each of these concepts is explained below.

***One-Transaction Concept* (*Cost Method*).** Under this approach the purchase and subsequent resale of treasury stock is viewed as comprising *one continuous capital transaction;* that is, measurement (and recording) of the net effect of the treasury stock transactions on the various elements of capital are deferred until resale. This method frequently is referred to as the *cost method,* in view of the fact that the *treasury stock account is carried at cost.* The following illustration indicates the accounting treatment to be accorded treasury stock under the cost method.

a. To record the initial sale (at organization) of 10,000 shares of common stock, par $25, at $26 per share:

Cash	260,000	
Common stock (10,000 shares at $25 par value)		250,000
Contributed capital in excess of par ($1 per share)		10,000

b. To record a subsequent repurchase of 1,000 shares of the common stock at $28 per share; the treasury stock acquired is recorded at *cost* as follows:

Treasury stock—common (1,000 shares at $28)	28,000	
Cash		28,000

c. To record a later sale of 500 shares of the treasury stock at $28 per share; note that this is the same as the purchase price, hence there is no "difference" to be given recognition. The 500 shares are removed from the treasury stock account at cost.[1]

Cash	14,000	
Treasury stock—common (500 shares at $28)		14,000

d. Now assume instead that 500 shares of treasury stock were sold at $30 per share; that is, at $2 per share above the purchase cost. In this case the excess over cost must be recognized through a credit to a special *contributed capital* account:

Cash (500 shares × $30)	15,000	
Contributed capital, from sale of treasury stock in excess of cost (500 shares × $2)		1,000
Treasury stock—common (500 shares × $28)		14,000

e. Now assume again that 500 shares of treasury stock were sold, but this time at $22 per share; that is, at $6 per share less than cost. In this case the deficit is debited to either a special contributed capital account or to retained earnings, as discussed below:

Cash (500 shares × $22)	11,000	
Contributed capital (or Retained earnings) (500 shares × $6) . . .	3,000	
Treasury stock—common (500 shares × $28)		14,000

[1] When more than one cost per share is recorded in the treasury stock account, the unit costs should be "flowed out" on a Fifo or an average cost basis.

Answer frame 4[16]

1. False. Extraordinary items are identified jointly by (1) infrequency of occurrence and (2) unusual nature, in relation to the environment in which they occur.
2. False. Extraordinary gains and losses are both reported on the income statement.
3. False. Prior period adjustments are reported on the statement of *retained earnings* because, by their very nature (prior period), they were not reflected on the income statement to which they applied.
4. True. A quasi-reorganization requires that retained earnings be adjusted to a zero balance.

If you missed any of the above questions, reread Frame 4[16] before proceeding. You have completed Chapter 16. Turn to Chapter 17, page 24, and continue reading.

Frame 1[17] continued

From the above illustration it is clear that the one-transaction concept views the balance of the treasury stock account as an *unallocated reduction of total capital* (it is a negative amount listed in the capital section of the balance sheet), and that the *allocation* will be made when the treasury stock is sold. There is general agreement among accountants that when treasury stock is sold at an amount greater than cost, as in entry (*d*) on page 25, such amount must be credited to a special contributed capital account (never credited to Retained Earnings). However, there is no common agreement as to the proper accounting treatment to be accorded a reduction in net assets (loss of capital) such as illustrated in entry (*e*) on the previous page. The following treatments are the more common ones:

1. Charge the difference (loss of capital) to any existing contributed capital that is related to the same class of stock in the following order:
   a. First to capital arising from prior treasury stock transactions.
   b. Second to any contributed capital in excess of par related to the same class of stock, on a per-share basis.
2. Charge contributed capital with the pro rata amount per share of any premium (or discount) that was recorded on orignal sale of the stock, and charge any remaining deficit to Retained Earnings. For example, the last situation (*e*) illustrated would be recorded as follows under this procedure:

Cash	11,000	
Contributed capital in excess of par (500 shares at original premium of $1 per share)	500	
Retained earnings	2,500	
Treasury stock—common (500 shares × $28)		14,000

3. Charge the entire difference (lost capital) to Retained Earnings.

The first alternative is theoretically preferable because it most closely parallels a "source of capital" accounting; the third alternative is frequently used because of its simplicity.

Dual-Transaction Concept (Par-Value Method). Under this approach the purchase and subsequent resale of treasury stock are viewed as *two separate and distinct transactions.* Thus, under this concept there is a *final accounting* upon purchase of the treasury stock and a sale of new stock is recognized at resale. Consistent with this concept the *treasury stock account is carried at par value,* which provides the basis for the frequent designation of it as the "par-value method." The following entries and explanations (utilizing the same data as above) are given to indicate the appropriate accounting treatment to be accorded treasury stock under the par-value method.

a. To record the initial sale (at organization) of 10,000 shares of common stock, par $25, at $26 per share:

Cash	260,000	
Common stock (10,000 shares at $25 par value)		250,000
Contributed capital in excess of par ($1 per share)		10,000

b. To record a subsequent repurchase of 1,000 shares of the common stock at $28 per share; the treasury stock is recorded at par value, as follows:

Treasury stock—common (1,000 shares at $25 par)	25,000	
Contributed capital in excess of par (1,000 shares at $1 original premium)	1,000	
Retained earnings	2,000	
Cash		28,000

The debit of $2,000 to Retained Earnings is viewed as a liquidating dividend; hence it is appropriately charged to Retained Earnings.

c. To record a later sale of 500 shares of the treasury stock at $28 per share; that is, at the same price as the cost of the treasury stock. This transaction is recorded in the same manner as if it were an original sale:

Cash	14,000	
Treasury stock—common (500 shares at par)		12,500
Contributed capital in excess of par (500 shares at $3)[2]		1,500

d. Now assume instead that 500 shares of treasury stock were sold at $30; that is, $2 per share above the cost (and $5 above par). Again the resale is recorded as an initial sale:

Cash (500 × $30)	15,000	
Treasury stock—common (500 shares at par)		12,500
Contributed capital in excess of par (500 × $5)		2,500

e. Now assume again that the 500 shares of the treasury stock were sold, but this time at $22 per share; that is, $6 below cost and $3 below par.

Cash (500 × $22)	11,000	
Retained earnings ($25 − $22) × 500 shares	1,500	
Treasury stock—common (500 shares at par)		12,500

In this entry the debit to Retained Earnings is based upon the notion that there has been a form of dividend distribution and further, that no *discount* liability attaches to treasury stock when resold.

Accounting for Nopar-Value Treasury Stock. Nopar-value treasury stock with an assigned or stated value per share should be accounted for as illustrated above for par-value stock. With respect to true nopar-value stock, the cost method would be applied exactly as though the stock had a par value. Under the par-value method, average paid in per share may be substituted for par value.

Indicate whether each of the following statements is true or false by writing *T* or *F* in the space provided.

_______ 1. The overall effect on total capital is the same under the cost and par-value methods.

_______ 2. Net asset increases and decreases from treasury stock transactions affect retained earnings.

_______ 3. Treasury stock purchased by a corporation in order to meet obligations involving issuance of its stock may in some restricted circumstances be properly classified as an asset.

_______ 4. Upon purchase of treasury stock accounted for under the cost method, preexisting equities pertaining to the treasury shares are removed from the accounts.

Now check your responses by comparing them with Answer Frame 1[17], page 28.

[2] Some accountants prefer to use the account designation, Contributed Capital from Treasury Stock Transactions; it would be reported under the *same* subcategory of capital on the balance sheet as "Contributed capital in excess of par."

Answer frame 1[17]

1. True. Only subcategories of capital are affected differently under the two methods.
2. False. Increases affect contributed capital. Decreases affect contributed capital and/or retained earnings.
3. False. Treasury stock is never an asset because it is a shrinkage in the size of the corporation. Therefore, it is negative (contra) capital.
4. False. This characterizes the par-value method in which premium (per share) is removed upon acquisition to reflect the cessation of the original equity. Under the cost method, preexisting equities are not removed until the treasury stock cycle is completed, that is, when treasury stock is subsequently resold.

If you missed any of the above questions, reread Frame 1[17] before proceeding. Then turn to Frame 2[17], below, and continue reading.

Frame 2[17]

Restriction of Retained Earnings for Cost of Treasury Stock

Since treasury stock purchases result in disbursement of the assets of a corporation to the shareholders (whether or not there is a balance in Retained Earnings), creditors' interests could be placed in jeopardy. In Chapter 15 it was noted that the concept of legal capital is concerned in part with the protection of creditor interests; another law with the same objective limits the maximum amount of treasury stock that may be held at any one time to the balance in retained earnings. A number of states have such laws because they afford some protection to creditors in that they constitute a restriction on retained earnings equivalent to the cost of all treasury stock held, thereby reducing the amount that may be legally declared as dividends. For example, a corporation having a balance in Retained Earnings of $30,000 and holding treasury stock costing $25,000 could declare only $5,000 in dividends. The restriction on retained earnings must be reported on the balance sheet; accordingly, in such situations it is desirable that the following additional entry be made when the treasury stock is purchased:

Retained earnings	25,000	
Retained earnings appropriated for cost of treasury stock held . . .		25,000

When the treasury stock is sold the above entry is reversed.

Reporting Treasury Stock on the Balance Sheet

Treasury stock must be reported on the balance sheet in accordance with the full-disclosure principle. Treasury shares do not carry any of the basic rights listed on page 2. Treasury stock is not an investment, as are shares owned in *other* corporations; rather it is a *reduction* in the capital section of the balance sheet. The preferred way of reporting treasury stock is indicated in Illustrations 17–1 (when carried at cost) and 17–2 (when carried at par value).

Illustration 17–1

Assumption: Treasury Stock Accounted for at Cost (one-transaction concept)

Stockholders' Equity

Contributed Capital:		
Capital stock, par value $25, 10,000 shares authorized and issued of which 500 shares are held as treasury stock		$250,000
Other contributed capital:		
In excess of par		10,000
Total Contributed Capital		260,000
Retained Earnings:		
Appropriated equal to cost of treasury stock	$14,000	
Unappropriated	16,000	30,000
Total		290,000
Less: Cost of treasury stock (500 shares)		14,000
Total Capital		$276,000

Illustration 17–2

Assumption: Treasury Stock Accounted for at Par Value (dual-transaction concept)

Stockholders' Equity

Contributed Capital:		
Capital stock, par value $25, 10,000 shares authorized and issued		$250,000
Less: Treasury stock, 500 shares at par $25		12,500
Total Capital Stock Outstanding, 9,500 shares		237,500
Other contributed capital:		
In excess of par		10,500
Total Contributed Capital		248,000
Retained Earnings:		
Appropriated for cost of treasury stock held	$14,000	
Unappropriated	14,000	28,000
Total Capital		$276,000

Retirement of Stock

A corporation may purchase some of its own stock for the purpose of immediate retirement; laws generally permit such action even though the stock is not *callable,* provided creditor interests are not jeopardized. When stock is retired, all capital items relating to the specific shares are removed from the accounts, any deficit of cost over per-share amount of paid-in capital is debited to Retained Earnings as a form of dividends, and any "gain" is recorded as a credit in an appropriately designated contributed capital account. To illustrate, assume the following account balances:

Common stock, 10,000 shares, par $50	$500,000
Contributed capital in excess of par ($4 per share)	40,000

Situation 1—Assume 1,000 shares of the common is purchased at $60 per share and retired; the entry would be:

Common stock (1,000 shares × $50 par)	50,000	
Contributed capital in excess of par, common (1,000 × $4)	4,000	
Retained earnings	6,000	
Cash (1,000 shares × $60)		60,000

Situation 2—Assume instead that the 1,000 shares were purchased at $45 per share and retired; the entry would be:

Common stock (1,000 shares × $50)	50,000	
Contributed capital in excess of par, common (1,000 × $4)	4,000	
Contributed capital, from retirement of common stock		9,000
Cash (1,000 shares × $45)		45,000

Conversion of Stock

Corporations occasionally issue *convertible* stock which permits the shareholder, under specified conditions, to exchange his or her shares for shares of other classes of stock. In recording a conversion, the capital related to the old shares is removed and the capital related to the new shares is recorded. To illustrate, assume the following account balances before conversion:

Preferred stock, 6%, par $100, 5,000 shares outstanding	$ 500,000
Contributed capital in excess of par, preferred ($2 per share)	10,000
Common stock, par $50, 100,000 shares authorized, of which 40,000 shares are outstanding	2,000,000
Contributed capital in excess of par, common ($5 per share)	200,000

Now assume that a shareholder turns in 1,000 shares of preferred stock. Under the conversion privilege, two shares of common are issued for each share of preferred turned in. The entry would be:

Preferred stock (1,000 shares × $100 par)	100,000	
Contributed capital in excess of par, preferred (1,000 × $2)	2,000	
Common stock (2,000 shares × $50)		100,000
Contributed capital from conversion of preferred stock		2,000

Determine whether each of the following statements is true or false.

_______ 1. Legal restrictions on retained earnings for the purchase of treasury stock serve to protect creditor equity holders.

_______ 2. No cash or stock dividends are ever paid on treasury stock.

_______ 3. When treasury stock is retired, there is a reduction in total assets and a reduction in total stockholders' equity.

_______ 4. Total stockholders' equity is not changed by the conversion of preferred stock into common stock.

Now check your responses by comparing them with Answer Frame 2[17], page 32.

Frame 3[17]

Stock Rights

A corporation may extend *stock rights* to certain individuals. These rights permit them to acquire shares of stock under specified conditions, and usually at a potentially favorable price. Stock rights are evidenced by certificates generally known as *stock warrants*. Subject to specified restrictions, stock rights may be bought and sold on the market and frequently have a quoted price. Stock rights from the investor's point of view will be discussed in Chapter 18; the discussion to follow considers them from the point of view of the *issuing corporation.* A stock warrant (right) specifies (*a*) the option price for the share, (*b*) the number of rights required to obtain a new share of stock, and (*c*) expiration date of the right. When stock rights are issued on the basis of shares of stock already owned, one right is issued per share owned.

Situations in which stock rights are issued include:

1. Special concessions to present shareholders in order to raise capital.
2. To enhance the marketability of other issues such as bonds payable or preferred stock.
3. As compensation to outsiders such as underwriters.
4. As additional compensation to executives and other employees (usually referred to as stock options).

In the case of special concessions to stockholders, only a memorandum entry needs to be made on the issue date. This facilitates preparation of the balance sheet footnote to disclose the number of stock rights outstanding.

In the case of stock rights offered with bonds payable or preferred stock, the stock rights may or may not be detachable (i.e., separable from the bonds or preferred stock). If they are detachable, it is likely that there will be a separate market for the stock rights. At the time of issuing the bonds (plus stock rights), the credits should be apportioned between the two equities on the basis of relative market values. If the stock rights are not detachable, there will exist no basis on which to make the apportionment. Accordingly, the stock rights are ignored in recording issuance of the bonds, and then the stock is recorded in the normal manner when the rights are exercised. However, a memorandum entry should be made at the time the bonds are issued with rights to note that the stock rights have been issued and are outstanding.

The last two situations listed above are sufficiently similar that they will both be illustrated using the case of stock options for employees. *APB Opinion No. 25* identifies two types of option plans: compensatory and noncompensatory. As the names imply, the former is a form of compensation, usually for executives, while the latter allows employees to purchase stock at a modest discount, generally approximating security commissions.

Accounting for noncompensatory plans is substantially the same as the case of special concessions to stockholders.

Accounting for compensatory plans can be somewhat more complicated, depending on the specific provisions of the option plan. The compensation is equal to the difference between the market price of the stock at measurement date and the option price multiplied by the number of shares under option. The complications arise when executives earn the options in one period and the amount of compensation is determined in another period. In view of these complications, *Opinion No. 25* identifies as the measurement date (i.e., the date on which the compensation is measured) the earliest date on which are known both: (1) the number of optioned shares and (2) the option price.

To illustrate a relatively simple case, assume that the measurement date is the grant date, executives have earned the options during the current period, and on the grant date:

Market price of stock	$25
Option price	$20
Par value	$10
Number of option shares per executive	1,000
Number of executives	5

a. The following entry would be made to record the compensation:

	Debit	Credit
Executive compensation expense (5 × 1,000 × ($25 − $20))	25,000	
Executive stock options outstanding—common		25,000

The expense account is an operating expense, and the stock options account is an element of stockholders' equity.

Answer frame 2[17]

1. True. The restrictions on retained earnings affords the creditors some protection by the limitation on the purchase of treasury stock. In the absence of such a limitation, the company could pay out all the assets to stockholders by buying back their shares and the creditors would be left with no assets to satisfy their claims.
2. True. Treasury stock does not carry any of the basic rights associated with outstanding stock, including the right to participate in a declared dividend; therefore, no cash or stock dividends would be paid.
3. False. The retirement of treasury stock eliminates the treasury stock account (a contra capital account) and also reduces the regular stock account (a positive capital account); therefore, there is no change in total assets or total stockholders' equity.
4. True. The conversion of stock does not affect total capital. It merely changes the composition thereof.

If you missed any of the above questions, reread Frame 2[17] before proceeding. Then turn to Frame 3[17], page 30, and continue reading.

Frame 3[17] continued

b. Now assume that on the date the options expire, four of the executives exercise their options and the fifth allows his options to lapse. The related entry is:

Cash (4 × 1,000 × $20)	80,000	
Executive stock options outstanding—common	25,000	
Common stock (4 × 1,000 × $10)		40,000
Contributed capital in excess of par, common (4 × 1,000 × ($20 − $10)) + (⅘ × $25,000)		60,000
Contributed capital—lapse of stock options (⅕ × $25,000)		5,000

In the event that the measurement date is subsequent to the date on which Executive Compensation Expense must be recognized, *Opinion No. 25* requires that estimates of market price, option price, and number of option shares be made and that the compensation be accrued based on the estimate. Then on the measurement date, the total actual compensation is computed and any remaining compensation expense must be prorated to the current and future periods to the extent that it has not already been recognized.

Work the following problem for a company with two executives and a December 31 year-end. Basic data for stock option plan:

Grant date	January 1, 1977
Measurement date	June 30, 1978
Expiration date	January 1, 1980

Number of executives covered by the plan—2
Compensation to be earned evenly over 1977–79

	Estimates of Measurement Date Data		*Actual Data*
	On 1/1/77	*On 12/31/77*	*on 6/30/78*
Market price per share	$35	$37	$39
Option price per share	$31	$31	$31
Number of option shares per executive	100	100	100

How much compensation expense will the company recognize for 1977? 1978? 1979?
Now compare your answer with the solution given in Answer frame 3[17], page 34.

Frame 4[17]

Earnings per Share

The earnings per share (EPS) of common stock has great importance to investors because it is an important statistic in measuring the operating performance of the corporation. In its simplest form, EPS is simply the periodic net income divided by the number of shares of common stock outstanding for the period (i.e., net income/number shares outstanding). Most corporations have one or more of the following factors that complicate the computation of EPS:

1. Outstanding nonconvertible preferred stock (in addition to common).
2. Additional issues of common stock during the period.
3. Outstanding common stock rights or options (hereafter labeled stock options).
4. Convertible securities such as bonds payable or preferred stock, which are convertible to common (hereafter labeled convertibles).

Presence of the first two items listed requires straightforward adjustments to the basic formula given above. For example, the corporation with preferred stock outstanding has an ongoing dividend requirement unless the preferred stock is specified as noncumulative. Therefore, it is necessary to reduce net income by any cumulative preferred dividends whether or not the dividends are declared.

The issue of additional common shares during the period simply requires that the corporation divide net income by the weighted average number of shares outstanding for the period.

Basic Concepts

Concepts which are unique to EPS computations and which form the principal basis for the discussion to follow are:

1. Simple and complex capital structures.
2. Common stock equivalents (CSEs).
3. Primary EPS and fully diluted EPS.
4. Dilution and antidilution.

If only the complicating Factors 1 and 2 above (i.e., preferred stock and additional issues of common stock) are present, the capital structure is classified by *APB Opinion No. 15* as *simple,* whereas the presence of Factors 3 and 4 give rise to a *complex* capital structure. The added complexity arises due to the facts that (*a*) stock options and convertible securities are not shares of common stock, but (*b*) there is the possibility that they may become shares of common and hence dilute the EPS. *Opinion No. 15* on "Earnings per Share" is heavily influenced by the exception principle of conservatism, as evidenced by the attention given to dilution.

Opinion No. 15 requires that tests be performed to determine whether it is probable that stock options and convertibles will become common stock during the current period. If the test results are affirmative, then the item in question is labeled a common stock equivalent (CSE) and used in computing *primary EPS.*

If the test result with respect to *stock options* is negative, stock options are ignored in all EPS computations. If the test results with respect to *convertibles* are negative, then convertibles are ignored in computing *primary* EPS. However, unlike stock options, convertibles are not dismissed altogether if they fail to qualify as CSEs.

An additional test is performed to determine whether convertibles not qualifying as *CSEs* will nevertheless be *dilutive* (i.e., if conversion into common would reduce EPS) or *antidilutive* (i.e., would increase EPS). If the convertibles are deemed to be *dilutive,* they are used in computing *fully diluted EPS.* If they are *antidilutive,* they are ignored altogether, and *primary* and *fully diluted EPS* are the same.

Answer frame 3^{17}

1977 compensation:
Use 12/31/77 estimates. (2 × 100 × ($37 − $31)) ÷ 3 years = $400

1978 compensation:
Use 6/30/78 actual data. 2 × 100 × ($39 − $31) = $1,600 total compensation − $400 recognized in 1977 = $1,200 compensation. $1,200 compensation ÷ 2 (for 1978 and 1979) = $600

1979 compensation:
$1,600 total − ($400 + $600) = $600

If you missed any part of this problem, reread Frame 3^{17} before proceeding. Then turn to Frame 4^{17}, page 33, and continue reading.

Frame 4^{17} continued

The tests performed to determine whether stock options and convertibles qualify as *CSEs* are as follows:

1. If the average market price of the stock for the period exceeds the option price, this suggests that there is a high probability that the options will be exercised and hence become shares of common stock. The options are therefore classified as *CSEs.*
2. If the true yield interest rate on the convertible bonds is less than two thirds the prime interest rate at the time the bonds were issued, this suggests that the bonds were bought substantially for the convertibility option rather than for the interest yield. Accordingly, these bonds are classified as *CSEs* because it appears likely that the bonds will be converted into common stock.

To illustrate EPS computations, assume that a corporation has the following basic data and a December 31 year-end:

Common stock, par $10, 90,000 shares outstanding at January 1 and 6,000 additional shares issued on May 1	$900,000
Preferred stock, par $20, 6% nonconvertible, 2,500 shares outstanding all year	$ 50,000
Common stock warrants outstanding all year (for 2,000 shares):	
Option price of stock	$20
Average market price of the stock for the current period	$25
Convertible bonds payable, 6% (each $1,000 bond convertible into 40 shares of common stock)	$100,000
Bond price at time of issuance of bonds payable	$120,000
Bank prime interest rate	7%
Income before extraordinary items	$120,000
Extraordinary loss (net of 45% average income tax)	($10,000)
Net income	$110,000

The *first* step in computing EPS is to identify the basic EPS number, temporarily ignoring the stock options and convertible bonds. Income before extraordinary items less preferred dividends is divided by the weighted average number of common shares outstanding during the year:

$$\frac{\$120{,}000 - .06(\$50{,}000)}{(90{,}000 \times 4/12) + (96{,}000 \times 8/12)} = \frac{\$117{,}000}{94{,}000} = \$1.25$$

The *second* step involves (*a*) recognition of the complex capital structure arising from the stock options and convertibles and (*b*) the tests to determine whether they qualify as CSEs.

1. Stock options—Because the average market price exceeds the option price, they are CSEs. The adjustment to the above computations involves the assumption that the corporation will take the cash proceeds from exercise of the options and purchase an equal number of treasury shares at the average price of the stock for the period. The difference between the number of shares issued

less the number of shares treated as though they were repurchased is then added to the (denominator) number of shares outstanding to compute primary EPS. This method, referred to in *Opinion No. 15* as the *treasury stock method,* is illustrated below:

2,000 new shares
× $20 option price
$40,000 proceeds
÷ $25 average market price
1,600 shares of treasury stock can be purchased

2,000 shares − 1,600 shares = 400 additional (dilutive) shares

2. Convertible bonds—prime rate test:

$$\frac{.06(\$100{,}000)}{\$120{,}000} = 5\% \text{ true yield interest rate on bonds}$$

Bank prime rate: .07 × ⅔ = 4.67%

The convertible bonds are *not* CSEs because the yield rate exceeds two thirds of the prime interest rate. Therefore, the bonds are not used in computing primary EPS. However, it will later be necessary to determine whether the bonds are *dilutive,* in which case they will be used to compute fully diluted EPS.

The *third* step is to compute primary EPS. Based on the results of the tests for CSEs, it is necessary to modify the basic EPS computation given in the first step in order to give effect to the stock options, which are CSEs.

$$\frac{\$117{,}000}{94{,}000 + 400} = \frac{\$117{,}000}{94{,}400} = \$1.24$$

Primary EPS will then be reported on the income statement of the corporation in the following manner:

Income before extraordinary items:	$\frac{\$117{,}000}{94{,}000 + 400} = \frac{\$117{,}000}{94{,}400} =$	$1.24
Extraordinary loss:	$\frac{\$10{,}000}{94{,}400} =$	(.11)
Net income:	$\frac{\$107{,}000}{94{,}400} =$	$1.13

The *fourth* step is to perform the test to determine whether the convertible bonds are potentially dilutive. If they are, then the bonds will be used in computing fully diluted EPS; if not, they are ignored. In the event the bonds are dilutive and hence used in computing EPS, the adjustment to primary EPS will involve:

1. Adding back to net income the aftertax interest on the bonds, and
2. Incrementing the number of shares by the additional shares into which the bonds may be converted.

The test for dilution or antidilution then proceeds as follows. The quotient of aftertax interest divided by the number of additional shares (from converting the bonds) is compared to primary EPS. If the quotient is less than primary EPS, the bonds are dilutive and are used in computing fully diluted EPS. If the quotient is greater than primary EPS, the bonds are antidilutive and therefore ignored, in which case primary and fully diluted EPS are the same. The test proceeds as follows, assuming a 45 percent income tax rate:

$$\frac{.06(\$100{,}000)(1.00 - .45)}{100 \times 40} = \frac{\$3{,}300}{4{,}000} = \$.83$$

Because \$.83 is less than \$1.24, the bonds are dilutive and hence are used to compute fully diluted EPS.

The *fifth* and final step is to compute fully diluted EPS as follows:

Income before extraordinary items: $\frac{\$120{,}000 - \$3{,}000 + \$3{,}300}{94{,}000 + 400 + 4{,}000} = \$1.22$

Extraordinary loss: $\frac{\$10{,}000}{98{,}400} = \quad (.10)$

Net income: $\frac{\$110{,}000 - \$3{,}000 + \$3{,}300}{98{,}400} = \$1.12$

Work the following problem:

Show that the bonds would be antidilutive if each \$1,000 of them were convertible into 20 shares of common stock (instead of 40).

Now compare your answer with the solution given in Answer Frame 4[17], page 38.

chapter 18

LONG-TERM INVESTMENTS IN EQUITY SECURITIES

Frame 1[18]

Nature of Long-Term Investments

In Chapter 7, short-term investments were defined as (*a*) those having current marketability and (*b*) those that management intended to convert into cash in the near future. Thus, they were classified as current assets. In contrast, all investments that are intended to be held for longer periods (even if readily marketable) are classified as long-term investments. A special caption on the balance sheet "Investments and Funds" is used for reporting long-term investments. Long-term investments usually are comprised of bonds and/or shares of stock. Bonds held as long-term investments present special problems and are covered in Chapter 19; this chapter deals with long-term investments in stocks only. A company may own sufficient stock for a controlling interest in another corporation (say, over 50% of the outstanding shares), or it may own less than a controlling interest.

Cost of Long-Term Investments of Stocks

Shares of stock may be acquired on the security markets, directly from an individual, or directly from the issuing corporation. *Cost* is the basis for initial recording of long-term investments. Cost includes, in addition to the purchase price, such expenditures as brokerage fees, excise taxes, and other transfer costs incurred by the purchaser. Interest paid when shares are purchased "on credit" should not be considered as a part of the cost but as interest expense. When noncash considerations (such as a machine) are given for shares of stock, the *cost* assigned to the investment should be either the fair market value of the consideration given or the fair market value of the shares received, whichever is the more definitely determinable. Expected future dividends are not recognized (accrued) when stock is purchased as an investment.

Accounting for Long-Term Investments in Stocks

There are four generally accepted methods of accounting for long-term investments in stock: (*a*) cost, (*b*) equity, (*c*) consolidation, and (*d*) market value. The consolidation method involves many specific considerations which are covered extensively in a later accounting course and accordingly are not covered in this book. The market value method is generally accepted only for enterprises which maintain large permanent investments in stocks, such as insurance companies and mutual funds.

In determining whether the cost method or the equity method is appropriate, two items need to be considered. First, if the investment is *nonvoting* stock, the investor company cannot significantly influence the actions of the investee (the other) company. In this case, the cost method must be used. Second, if the investment is *voting* stock, the determining factor is the level of ownership in the investee company. The table below presents the situations in which each method is appropriate:

Investment Characteristics	*Level of Ownership*	*Accounting Method*
A. No significant influence or control:		
1. Nonvoting stock owned	All levels	Cost
2. Voting stock owned	Less than 20%	Cost
B. Significant influence but not control:		
3. Voting stock owned	20% up to 50%	Equity
C. Controlling interest:		
4. Voting stock owned but for special reasons not appropriate to consolidate .	Over 50%	Equity
5. Voting stock owned, appropriate to consolidate	Over 50%	Consolidation

Under all methods, a long-term investment is initially recorded at cost when it is purchased. Subsequent to purchase, however, the accounting differs for the cost, equity, and market value methods.

Cost Method

The *cost* method can more appropriately be termed the lower-of-cost-or-market (LCM) method insofar as it is applied. FASB *Statement No. 12,* which is pertinent to valuing investments, specifies, among other things, that:

1. Temporary market value declines are recorded as a reduction in the book value of the investment account, usually via a credit to an allowance (valuation) account. Declines of this nature are recorded as negative unrealized capital and reported in the stockholders' equity section of the balance sheet.
2. The LCM determination must be applied separately to long-term and short-term investment portfolios. Thus, the *portfolio* is the *investment* unit for valuation purposes.
3. Permanent market value declines are treated as though they were realized losses. That is, the investment account is written down directly and a loss is recognized. This lower market value is used as a new cost basis for future LCM determinations.
4. Market value increases are recorded only up to a maximum, equal to the investment original cost.
5. Cash dividends received on investment shares are recognized as revenue.

Answer frame 4[17]

Computations:

$$\frac{.06\ (\$100{,}000)\ (1.00 - .45)}{100 \times 20} = \frac{\$3{,}300}{2{,}000} = \$1.65$$

Because $1.65 is greater than primary EPS (before extraordinary items) of $1.24, it is clear that addition of $3,300 to the numerator and 2,000 (additional shares) to the denominator of the EPS computation would increase EPS above $1.24. This increase is the nature of *antidilution.*

If you missed the answer, reread Frame 4[17] before proceeding. Then continue reading Chapter 18, page 36.

Frame 1[18] continued

To illustrate the cost method, assume that a corporation acquired for cash, on January 1, 19A, the following long-term investments, each less than 20% of the outstanding shares of the investee companies:

X Corporation, 5,000 voting shares at $12 per share	=	$ 60,000
Y Corporation, 4,000 nonvoting shares at $20 per share	=	80,000
		$140,000

The entry to record the acquisition would be:

Long-term investment in stocks (at cost)	140,000	
Cash		140,000

On December 31, 19A, the following market quotes were available: X Corporation stock, $10; Y Corporation stock, $21. On this date, Y Corporation paid a cash dividend of $.50 per share. The entry to record the temporary market value decline in the portfolio would be:

Unrealized loss on long-term investment in stocks	6,000	
Allowance to reduce long-term investment in stocks to market		6,000

Computations:

Investee	*Shares*	*Cost*		*Market*		*Balance in Allowance Account*
X	5,000	$ 60,000		$ 50,000		
Y	4,000	80,000		84,000		
Aggregate portfolio		$140,000	–	$134,000	=	$6,000

The entry to record the receipt of the dividend would be:

Cash ($.50 × 4,000)	2,000	
Investment revenue		2,000

On August 10, 19B, the investor unexpectedly sold 1,000 shares of the Y Corporation stock at $24. The entry would be:

Cash ($24 × 1,000)	24,000	
Long-term investment in stocks ($20 × 1,000)		20,000
Realized gain on sale of long-term investment		4,000

On December 31, 19B, the market value of X stock is $10.50 per share, and the market value of Y stock is $22 per share. The entry to record the increase in market value is:

Allowance to reduce long-term investment in stocks to market	4,500	
Unrealized loss on long-term investment in stocks		4,500

Computations:

Investee	Shares	Cost		Market		Balance in Allowance Account
X	5,000	$ 60,000		$ 52,500		
Y	3,000	60,000		66,000		
Aggregate Portfolio		$120,000	–	$118,500	=	$1,500
Balance in allowance account prior to current adjustment						6,000
Reduction needed to adjust allowance account						$4,500

If the decline in the market value of the X stock at December 31, 19B, had been permanent, the entry to record the decline would have been:

Loss on market value of long-term investment in stocks	7,500	
Long-term investment in stocks (5,000 × ($12 – $10.50)) . .		7,500

This permanent loss, unlike the unrealized (temporary) loss which is reported on the balance sheet, should be reported on the income statement. On the next financial statement date, the *new* cost of $10.50 per share of X stock would be used for determining the lower of cost or market.

True or false?

_______ 1. Cost, equity, and market value methods are acceptable alternative methods of accounting for a 35% investment in nonvoting stock.

_______ 2. Under all of the above methods, the investment is initially recorded at cost.

_______ 3. Under the cost method, market value increases are never recognized.

Work the following problem:

_______ 4. A long-term investment in 100 shares of nonvoting stock was purchased for $1,500. One year later the investee company paid a $1 per share cash dividend. At that time its stock was quoted at $13 per share.

At the end of the second year, the stock of the investee company was quoted at $15.50 per share. No dividends were paid during the second year.

a. How much investment revenue should the investor report for each year?

b. At what amount would the investment be reported at the end of each of the two years?

c. How much unrealized gain or loss would the investor report on the balance sheet at the end of each of the two years?

Now compare your answers with those given in Answer Frame 1[18], page 40.

Frame 2[18]

Equity Method

The equity method recognizes a special relationship between the investor company and the investee (i.e., the other) company. This relationship results from the 20%–50% ownership of the investee by the in-

Answer frame 1[18]

1. False. Only cost and market value methods are acceptable alternatives because the stock is nonvoting. Market value is acceptable only for investment-oriented companies.
2. True. Long-term investments are initially recorded at cost.
3. False. Market value increases are recognized up to a maximum, equal to the investment cost, regardless of the method of accounting used.
4. *a.* Since the cost method must be used, only dividends received are recorded as revenue. Therefore, 100 shares × $1 = $100 investment revenue is reported in the first year and none in the second year.

   b. Under the cost method the investment is reported at LCM (equals market in this case) of $1,300 at the end of Year 1 and at LCM (equals original cost) of $1,500 at the end of Year 2.

   c. Unrealized loss is $200 at the end of Year 1, and there is no unrealized gain or loss at the end of Year 2. It is important to note in this case that because the market value of the investment rose to a value in excess of cost by the end of Year 2, an entry would have been made in Year 2 to eliminate the balances in both the allowance account and the unrealized loss account.

If you missed any of the above, reread Frame 1[18] before proceeding. Then continue reading Frame 2[18], page 39.

Frame 2[18] continued

vestor, which suggests that the investor company can significantly influence the affairs of the investee company. *APB Opinion No. 18* specifies, among other things, that the investor should:

1. Recognize, as investment revenue, the investor's proportionate share of the income of the other company and increase the investment account by the same amount.
2. Record cash dividends received on investment shares as reductions in the investment account, because the dividend declared by the other company reduces the investor's equity (i.e., the investment) in the investee.
3. Record additional depreciation on the investor's cost of the depreciable assets of the investee that exceed the investee's cost of such assets.
4. Record amortization of any purchased goodwill implicit in the purchase price of the investment.

To illustrate the equity method, assume that P Company paid $9,000 for 40% of the outstanding voting common stock of S Company at a time when the following data were pertinent to S Company's balance sheet:

Assets not subject to depreciation	$13,000
Depreciable assets	12,000
	$25,000
Liabilities	$10,000
Stockholders' equity	15,000
	$25,000

Also, on the date P Company made the investment, S Company's depreciable assets had a fair market value of $14,000. All other assets had current market values equal to their book values. All long-term assets, both tangible and intangible, have estimated lives of ten years. During the current year, S Company earned $4,000 of net income and declared a cash dividend on December 31 (year-end for both companies) of $1,500.

To record P Company's acquisition of 40% of the common stock of S Company:

Long-term investment in Company S stock	9,000	
Cash		9,000

To recognize P Company's proportionate share of the net income reported by S Company:

Long-term investment in Company S stock	1,600	
Investment revenue (.40 × $4,000)		1,600

To recognize additional depreciation on fixed asset cost paid by P Company in the acquisition price of S Company:

Investment revenue (.40 ($14,000 − $12,000)/10)	80	
Long-term investment in Company S stock		80

To recognize amortization of the goodwill implicit in the $9,000 acquisition price:

Investment revenue	220	
Long-term investment in Company S stock		220

Computations:

Acquisition price		$9,000
Fair market value of identifiable net assets acquired:		
Not depreciable (same as book value)	$13,000	
Depreciable assets	14,000	
Less: Liabilities	(10,000)	
Net assets at fair market value	17,000	
Ownership percentage	.40	
Fair market value of identifiable net assets acquired		6,800
Goodwill purchased		2,200
Estimated useful life		÷ 10
Annual goodwill amortization amount		$ 220

To record the declaration of the cash dividend by S Company:

Dividend receivable (.40 × $1,500)	600	
Long-term investment in Company S stock		600

Thus, for the current year, P Company would report the following:

Income Statement:	
Investment revenue ($1,600 − $80 − $220)	$1,300
Balance Sheet:	
Investments and Funds:	
Investment in Company S stock, equity basis (cost, $9,000) ($9,000 + $1,600 − $80 − $220 − $600)	$9,700

Answer the following questions on the equity method:

1. Explain why dividends received on investment shares accounted for on the equity basis are not recognized as revenue by the investor.
2. Why should the investor record additional depreciation on the investment?

Work the following problem on the equity method:

Refer to the basic facts given above in the illustration on the equity method. Alter those facts as follows:

a. Let the cost of the investment be $10,000.

b. Let the market value of the depreciable assets be $16,000.

c. All other facts are as given in the illustration.

3. How much goodwill did the investor purchase?
4. How much investment revenue should the investor report for the year?
5. What is the carrying value of the investment at the end of the year?

Now compare your responses with those given in Answer Frame 2[18], page 42.

Answer frame 2[18]

1. Dividends received on investments in stock accounted for at equity represent a type of liquidation of the investment in the sense that the investor converted part of the investment into cash. As a result, the investee company is smaller, and hence the investor's equity in the investee is reduced. Therefore, rather than representing revenue, the dividends represent a reduction in the investment account.
2. Because the investor is paying the current market value for the investment, this purchase price includes the current market value of the identifiable assets, some of which are depreciable. The other company is already depreciating its own cost of the depreciable assets, but only their own cost. Therefore, the investor must record additional depreciation to the extent that a higher (implicit) price was paid for the proportionate share of the depreciable assets of the investee.
3. Goodwill is $2,400, computed as follows:

Acquisition price of 40% investment		$10,000
Fair market value of net assets ($13,000 + $16,000 − $10,000)	$19,000	
Investor's proportionate ownership	× .40	7,600
Goodwill purchased		$ 2,400

4. Investment revenue is $1,200, computed as follows:

40% of investee's net income of $4,000		$1,600
Less: Amortization of goodwill ($2,400 ÷ 10)	$240	
Additional depreciation [($16,000 − $12,000) ÷ 10] .40	160	400
Investment revenue		$1,200

5. Carrying value is $10,600, computed as follows:

Cost		$10,000
Add 40% of investee net income		1,600
Less: Goodwill amortization	$240	
Additional depreciation	160	
Dividends (.40 × $1,500)	600	(1,000)
Investment carrying value at year-end		$10,600

If you missed any of the above questions, reread Frame 2[18]. Then continue reading Frame 3[18], below.

Frame 3[18]

Market Value Method

As indicated above, the market value method is generally accepted only for companies in investment-oriented industries. However, the market value method is conceptually superior to virtually all alternatives because application of it requires that the investment account on the balance sheet be reported at the current market value of the asset. For most decisions involving the investment, the current market value is the most relevant valuation amount.

Many accountants believe that the market value method is also conceptually superior for purposes of income recognition because it provides for the recognition of gains and losses on the investment *when they occur* rather than when the investment is sold. As a result, it is difficult under the market value method to manipulate net income by selling investments merely to realize gains or losses. The important point is that the wealth of the investor company changes as the market value of its investments change, and not only when investments are sold. Many accountants believe that these changes in wealth represent bona fide income events and hence see the timing of the recognition of income as a distinct advantage of the market value method.

Critics of the market value method point to the volatility of stock prices and argue that reporting investments and investment revenue on a market value basis necessarily leads to an unstable asset base and an unstable earnings trend. They also argue that in many cases (e.g., when securities are not widely traded), market values are not available or cannot be objectively determined.

Another position contrary to the market value method is based on the belief that the completed arm's-length transaction is indeed the most important income-producing event. Thus, while the balance sheet may present more relevant information if investments are carried at market value, this position would favor recognizing gains or losses only when investments are sold. Following this line of reasoning, the offsetting credits or debits in the journal entry to adjust investments to market values are labeled as unrealized capital and reported as a separate item in the stockholders' equity section of the balance sheet. The unrealized capital is, by definition, not an element of net income and hence is not closed to Retained Earnings.

Due to the fairly recent adoption of the market value method, current practice is not uniform as to the treatment of the offsetting credits or debits (for market value "gains" and "losses"). Some companies report them as gains and losses on the income statement, while others report them as unrealized capital in the balance sheet. However companies deal with the offsetting credits or debits, practice is uniform with respect to accounting for cash dividends received as *Investment Revenue.*

True or false?

______ 1. Cash dividends received on investment shares accounted for at market value are treated in the same manner as cash dividends received on shares accounted for at cost.

______ 2. The two methods of accounting for market value gains and losses both produce the same amount of periodic net income.

______ 3. The two methods of accounting for market value gains and losses both produce the same amount of total stockholders' equity.

Answer the following question:

4. Assume that market value gains and losses are reported on the income statement. What is the chief advantage of the market value method from an income statement viewpoint? from a balance sheet viewpoint?

Now compare your responses with Answer Frame 3[18], page 44.

Frame 4[18]

Share Identification at Resale

It is not unusual for an investor to purchase several lots of the same security at different times and at different prices. For example, assume Company K purchased stock in Company S as follows: Month 1, 100 shares at $50 per share; Month 2, 200 shares at $60; and Month 3, 150 shares at $70. Assume further that in Month 6 it was decided to sell 200 shares at $80 per share. The entry would be:

Cash (200 shares @ $80)	16,000	
Investment in stock of S Company (Fifo basis) (100 shares × $50) + (100 shares × $60)		11,000
Gain on sale of investments		5,000

In the above entry the stocks were removed from the investment account on a *Fifo* basis; however, an *average* basis ($27,500 ÷ 450 shares = $61.11 per share) would have been acceptable. *Specific identifi-*

Answer frame 3[18]

1. True. Cash dividends are treated differently only under the equity method.
2. False. If market value gains (losses) are reported on the income statement, net income is greater (less) than net income if market value gains and losses are reported as unrealized capital in the balance sheet. In the former case, such gains (losses) impact on the Retained Earnings account of the balance sheet. In the latter case, the unrealized capital is listed as a separate line-item in the stockholders' equity section of the balance sheet, and Retained Earnings is not affected.
3. True. Only subdivisions of stockholders' equity are affected as described in 2 above.
4. If market value gains and losses are reported on the income statement, they are reported when they occur. By contrast, under other methods the cumulative effects of such gains and losses are reported only when the investment is disposed of. From a balance sheet viewpoint, the advantage is that the balance sheet reflects the current value of the investment. This is more relevant information for most decision-making purposes.

If you missed any of the above, reread Frame 3[18] before proceeding. Then continue reading Frame 4[18], page 43.

Frame 4[18] continued

cation of the shares sold is theoretically preferable; however, the gain could be "manipulated" through arbitrary selection of unit cost, and for this reason, Fifo or average cost is recommended.

Income from Stock Investments

Property Dividends. Assume that the investor, Corporation K, received a property dividend, say, ten shares of B Corporation, which S Corporation had acquired several years earlier as an investment. The stock in B Corporation is selling for $250 per share; the entry would be:

Investment in stock of B Corporation (10 shares @ $250)	2,500	
Investment revenue		2,500

Stock Dividends. Now assume that instead of receiving a property dividend the investor received a stock dividend from S Company. For every ten shares held, the investor received an additional share of common stock (par $100 per share), that is, a 10% stock dividend. In this case only a *memorandum* entry would be made as follows:

> Memorandum—On (date) received 100 shares S Company stock (par value $100 per share) as a stock dividend. New cost per share $81.82 ($90,000 ÷ 1,100 shares = $81.82).

Stock Splits. A stock split is effected when a corporation issues new or additional stock without "capitalizing" (debiting) retained earnings or otherwise adding to the amount of *legal capital;* in contrast, a stock dividend serves to *increase* legal capital (see Chapter 15). Now, assume that instead of receiving a cash dividend, the investor receives a stock split. For each share held, he or she receives an additional share (a 2 for 1 split). In this case, as with a stock dividend, a memorandum entry would be made:

> Memorandum—On (date) received 1,000 shares S Corporation stock (par value $50—note that the par value per share is affected by the stock split) as a stock split. The new cost per share is $45 ($90,000 ÷ 2,000 shares).

It is significant to note that in contrast to cash dividends and property dividends, the investor does *not* receive additional assets in the case of a stock dividend or a stock split; he or she only receives more shares and presumably the market value per share on the stock will decrease proportionately. At any rate, if market value per share does not decrease the investor cannot recognize any additional assets until the stock is sold.

Stock Rights on Investment Shares

A stock right is the privilege (evidenced by a *stock warrant*) to purchase stock of a specified corporation at a specified price in the future. There are a number of situations where stock warrants (rights) are issued. From the point of view of a long-term investment, a stock right frequently arises when the issuing corporation desires to raise additional capital by according current stockholders a priority. To illustrate, assume that Company P owns 1,000 shares of common stock (par value $50) in S Corporation which was acquired at $90 per share. Now assume the investor (Company P) receives a stock right for each share of common stock owned (1,000 shares) and that five rights plus $90 will purchase one new share of S Corporation stock. The investor (Company P) would record the receipt of the 1,000 rights by dividing the original cost ($90,000 debit in the investment account) between the rights and the stock as follows:

Investment in stock rights of S Corporation (1,000 × $1.76)	1,760	
Investment in common stock of S Corporation		1,760

Computation: Assuming the rights are being sold on the market at $2 each and the stock at $100 per share, exrights:
Allocation on basis of fair market value:

To one share of stock: (100/102) × $90	$88.24
To one stock right: (2/102) × $90	1.76
Total Cost per Share of Stock	$90.00

After this entry the *two* investment accounts would show the following balances:

Investment in common stock of S Corporation ($90,000 − $1,760) . .	$88,240
Investment in stock rights of S Corporation	1,760
Total	$90,000

Now assume two additional transactions take place as follows:

a. One half of the stock rights are exercised; that is, 500 are exercised:

Investment in stock of S Corporation (100 shares)	9,880	
Investment in rights of S Corporation (500 rights × $1.76)		880
Cash (100 shares × $90)		9,000

b. The other one half of the rights (500) are sold for $1.80 each:

Cash (500 rights × $1.80)	900	
Investment in rights of S Corporation (500 × $1.76)		880
Gain on sale of stock rights		20

Is each of the following statements true or false?

_______ 1. The date of declaration of a cash dividend is the date that the investor has first earned investment revenue.

_______ 2. A stock dividend represents income to the recipient.

_______ 3. In the case of a stock dividend or a stock split, other things being equal, the total market price of the shares outstanding shou'd not change.

_______ 4. Stock rights typically entitle the owner thereof to purchase specified shares of stock at reduced prices.

Now check your responses by comparing them with Answer Frame 4[18], page 46.

Answer frame 4[18]

1. True. On the declaration date, a legal obligation occurs for the corporation to pay cash to its shareholders.
2. False. Stock dividends simply represent more shares of the same (size) company. Therefore, stock dividends reduce investor's cost per share of stock.
3. True. It is presumed that the market price per share will react proportionately to a stock dividend or a stock split so that the total market value will be the same as before the dividend or split.
4. True. This statement defines stock rights.

If you missed any of the above questions, reread Frame 4[18] before turning to page 119 to work Examination 4. Then continue reading with Chapter 19 below.

chapter 19

ACCOUNTING FOR BONDS

Frame 1[19]

Nature of Bonds

A bond is a formal written contract to pay a specified sum (principal) at a designated maturity date, including a specified rate of interest over the duration of the indebtedness. Bonds are generally long-term debts and are issued by businesses and governmental units and other not-for-profit organizations. Necessarily there are two parties, the borrower who sells the bonds and the investor who purchases them. Accordingly, this chapter reviews the accounting problems for both parties; Part A considers the investor and Part B the borrower. To illustrate the similarity of the problems of the two parties, consider the following:

Books of Borrower, B Corporation			Books of Investor, I Corporation		

a. B Corporation sold bonds with maturity value of $10,000, due in 5 years, 8 percent interest payable annually, to I Corporation for $10,410.

Books of Borrower, B Corporation	Dr.	Cr.	Books of Investor, I Corporation	Dr.	Cr.
Cash	10,410		Investment in bonds—B Corporation	10,000	
Bonds payable		10,000	Premium on bond investment*	410	
Premium on bonds payable		410	Cash		10,410

* Frequently the premium (or discount) on bond investments is not recorded separately; in that case the investment account would be debited for $10,410 and amortization would be direct to the investment account.

b. Payment of annual interest and straight-line amortization of bond premium:

Interest expense	718		Cash	800	
Premium on bonds payable . .	82		Premium on bond investment . .		82
Cash		800	Interest revenue		718

Computations:
Cash interest: $10,000 × 8% = $800.
Premium amortization: $410 ÷ 5 years = $82 per year.

The above example assumed that I Corporation purchased the bonds as a long-term investment; hence, the premium was amortized. It will be recalled from Chapter 7 that short-term investments in bonds do not involve amortization since the holding period will be short.

Part A—Long-Term Investments in Bonds

Valuation of Long-Term Investments. Long-term investments should be classified on the balance sheet under the caption "Investments and Funds." At purchase, bonds are recorded at cost and any premium or discount is *amortized* over the *remaining* time that they are to be held (from date of purchase to date of maturity). Bonds normally are in denominations of $100, $1,000, and $10,000. Interest payments generally are semiannual, although the interest rate is quoted on an annual basis. Long-term investments in bonds are not reduced to lower of cost or market unless there clearly has been a permanent decline in value. The rate of interest paid by the borrower, as specified on the bond certificate, is known as the *nominal rate,* whereas the *yield rate* is the true rate of interest earned (the nominal and yield rate would be the same only when the bond sells at par). Yield rates are determined by the market rate of interest at the time the bonds are issued. In the preceding example the nominal rate was 8% per annum; since the bond sold at a premium, the yield rate was less than 8%. The premium (or discount) reflects the difference between the nominal and the yield rates of interest. The market usually quotes bonds on a *yield basis,* such as 4.2%. Thus, a $10,000 bond with a nominal rate of 5%, payable semiannually (i.e., each cash interest payment will be $10,000 × 2½% = $250), if purchased to yield 6% five years before maturity would cost $9,573.49 (a discount of $426.51). For a specified *yield* rate the selling price (valuation) of a bond is determined as follows:

V = (maturity amount × present value of 1) + (cash interest × present value of annuity of 1), both discounted at the effective yield rate.

The bond specified immediately above was valued as follows.

$$V = \$10{,}000 \times P_{\substack{n=10\\i=3\%}} + \$250 \times P_{\substack{n=10\\i=3\%}}$$
$$= (\$10{,}000 \times 0.74409391) + (\$250 \times 8.5302028) \text{ (Tables 6–2 and 6–4, respectively)}$$
$$= \$7{,}440.94 + \$2{,}132.55$$
$$= \$9{,}573.49.$$

Thus, a bond will sell for the sum of (1) the present value of the maturity value of the bond plus (2) the present value of the stream of interest receipts on the bond (each discounted at the yield rate).

Typically it is not necessary to perform the present value computation given above because special bonds tables are available, as shown in Illustration 19–1, that provide the basic *multiplier* for the various combinations of interest and time. The bond specified immediately above was valued as follows:

Table value for 5 years for 5% semiannual bond to yield 6% = .95734898 (per $1).
$10,000 × .95734898 = $9,573.49.

For all practical purposes, the table approach is used exclusively because of the ready availability of bond tables such as Illustration 19–1. It should be obvious that the bond multiplier is determined by the present value formula given above. The bond table is merely a derivative of the present value computation.

Illustration 19–1

Bond Table: Values to the Nearest Cent of a Bond for $1,000,000 at 5% Interest, Payable Semiannually

Yield or Net Income	*3 Years*	*3½ Years*	*4 Years*	*4½ Years*	*5 Years*
4.00 . .	1,028,007.65	1,032,359.96	1,036,627.41	1,040,811.19	1,044,912.93
4.85 . .	1,004,141.48	1,004,775.67	1,005,394.84	1,005,999.36	1,006.589.56
4.90 . .	1,002,758.67	1,003,180.75	1,003,592.72	1,003,994.85	1,004,387.36
4.95 . .	1,001,378.18	1,001,588.86	1,001,794.45	1,001,995.07	1,002,190.85
5.00 . .	1,000,000.00	1,000,000.00	1,000,000.00	1,000,000.00	1,000,000.00
5.25 . .	993,143.53	992,100.89	991,084.91	990,094.92	989,130.25
5.50 . .	986,344.08	984,276.48	982,264.21	980,305.80	978,399.81
5.75 . .	979,601.10	976,525.98	973,536.79	970,631.15	967,806.71
6.00 . .	972,914.05	968,848.59	964,901.54	961,069.45	957,348.98

Indicate whether each of the following statements is true or false by writing *T* or *F* in the space provided.

______ 1. A 5% bond purchased to yield 6% will be bought at a discount.

______ 2. Bond prices reflect present values of future cash flows discounted at the nominal interest rate.

3. Solve the following problem using (*a*) the formula and (*b*) the table. Compute the price of a 5% bond purchased to yield 5½% to maturity three years hence. Maturity value is $100,000, and interest is paid semiannually.

Now check your responses by comparing them with Answer Frame 1[19], page 50.

Frame 2[19]

Amortization of Bond Premium and Discount. The bond premium (or discount) must be amortized against the bond interest over the *remaining life* of the bonds. There are two widely used methods of computing the amortization, viz:

1. Straight-line amortization. The total premium or discount is simply prorated in equal dollar amounts to each time period between sale (or purchase) date and maturity date.
2. Interest method amortization. The total premium or discount is prorated, utilizing the interest (present value) concepts discussed in Chapter 6.

Straight-Line Amortization. Assume that on April 1, 1977, an investor purchased a 5%, $10,000 bond with three years of remaining life (2½% semiannual interest paid on March 31 and September 30 each year) for $10,280.08, the annual yield rate thus was 4%. If the straight-line amortization method is used, the entries for the remainder of the life of the bond investment would be as shown in Illustration 19–2. Alternatively, had the bond been purchased at a discount for $9,729.14, the entries would have been as shown in Illustration 19–3. In this case, the yield rate was 6% per annum.

Adjusting Entry for Bond Interest. When the books are to be adjusted and closed (end of the fiscal period) at a date *different* than the interest date on the bonds, an adjusting entry must be made to (*a*) accrue the interest since the last bond interest date and (*b*) amortize the premium (or discount) for the

Illustration 19–2

Premium Amortized by Straight-Line Method

Date	Cash Dr. (a)	Interest Revenue Cr. (b)	Premium on Bond Investment Cr. (c)	Investment Carrying Value (d)
4/1/77 . . .	—	—	—	$10,280.08
9/30/77 . . .	$250.00	$203.32	$ 46.68	10,233.40
3/31/78 . . .	250.00	203.32	46.68	10,186.72
9/30/78 . . .	250.00	203.32	46.68	10,140.04
3/31/79 . . .	250.00	203.32	46.68	10,093.36
9/30/79 . . .	250.00	203.32	46.68	10,046.68
3/31/80 . . .	250.00	203.32	46.68	10,000.00
			$280.08	

(*a*) $10,000 × 5% × 6/12 = $250.
(*b*) Cash interest $250 − $46.68 = $203.32.
(*c*) Total premium $280.08 ÷ 6 periods = $46.68. (This must be computed prior to computing (*b*) Interest Revenue.)
(*d*) Preceding carrying value minus the amortization of premium ($10,280.08 − $46.68 = $10,233.40).

Illustration 19–3

Discount Amortized by Straight-Line Method

Date	Cash Dr. (a)	Interest Revenue Cr. (b)	Discount on Bond Investment Dr. (c)	Investment Carrying Value (d)
4/1/77 . . .	—	—	—	$ 9,729.14
9/30/77 . . .	$250.00	$295.14	$ 45.14	9,774.28
3/31/78 . . .	250.00	295.14	45.14	9,819.42
9/30/78 . . .	250.00	295.14	45.14	9,864.56
3/31/79 . . .	250.00	295.14	45.14	9,909.70
9/30/79 . . .	250.00	295.14	45.14	9,954.84
3/31/80 . . .	250.00	295.16	45.16	10,000.00
			$270.86	

(*a*) $10,000 × 5% × 6/12 = $250.
(*b*) $250 + $45.14 = $295.14.
(*c*) $\frac{\$10,000 - \$9,729.14}{6}$ = $45.14. (This must be computed prior to computing (*b*) Interest Revenue.)
(*d*) $9,729.14 + $45.14 = $9,774.28.

same period of time. To illustrate, assume the investor in Illustration 19–2 closes the books on December 31. The following adjusting and closing entries would be required:

a. Adjusting entry for three months (October 1 to December 31, 1977):

Bond interest receivable (3/6 × $250)	125.00	
Premium on bond investment (or bond investment) (3/6 × $46.68) .		23.34
Bond interest revenue		101.66

This entry could be reversed on the first day of the next period.

b. Closing entry at December 31, 1977:

Bond interest revenue	304.98	
Income summary		304.98

Computation: $203.32 + $101.66 = $304.98.

Answer frame 1[19]

1. True. In order for a bond to yield a rate of interest in excess of its nominal rate, the purchaser must pay a price for the bond that is lower than the face value of the bond.
2. False. Bond prices reflect present value of future cash flows discounted at the present yield interest rate.
3. *a.*

$$V = \$100{,}000 \times \frac{1}{(1.0275)^6} + (\$100{,}000 \times .025) \times \frac{1 - \frac{1}{(1.0275)^6}}{.0275}$$
$$= (\$100{,}000 \times .8497849136) + (\$2{,}500 \times 5.462366778)$$
$$= \$98{,}634.41$$

b. $\$100{,}000 \times .98634408 = \$98{,}634.41$

If you missed any of the above questions, reread Frame 1[18] before proceeding. Then turn to Frame 2[19], page 48, and continue reading.

Frame 2[19] continued

Purchase of Bonds between Interest Dates. Frequently bonds are purchased between interest dates; in such situations part of the cash paid (i.e., the purchase price plus the accrued interest) is for the interest accrued since the last interest date. It must be remembered that at the next interest date after purchase the purchaser will receive interest for the *full* interest period, although the bonds were held less than that period, because issuers of bonds cannot feasibly split interest payments between owners. Therefore, the interest included in the cash paid must be recorded separately as an offset to interest revenue. To illustrate, assume an investor purchased $10,000 of 5% bonds on July 1, 1977 (see illustration 19–2); the bonds pay interest semiannually on March 31 and September 30. Thus, the investor had to pay for three months' accrued interest plus the cost of the bonds; the total price, including the accrued interest, was $10,381.73. The purchase would be recorded as follows:

	Debit	Credit
Bond investment	10,000.00	
Premium on bond investment	256.73*	
Interest revenue ($10,000 × 5% × 3/12)	125.00	
Cash		10,381.73

* ($10,280.07 + $10,233.39) ÷ 2 = $10,256.73, from Illustration 19–2.

Determine whether each of the following statements is true or false.

_______ 1. Refer to Illustration 19–3. For 1978, the amount of interest revenue that the investor would have recorded was $500.

_______ 2. Refer to Illustration 19–2. At the time the investor purchased the bonds, the market interest rate must have been less than the nominal rate on the bonds.

_______ 3. Straight-line amortization of premium or discount assumes a consistant interest rate on a bond carrying value that is changing due to the amortization toward maturity value.

_______ 4. When bonds are purchased between interest dates, it is customary for the seller to charge the buyer for accrued interest which (a) the seller has earned to date of sale and (b) the purchaser will collect in cash on the next interest date.

Now check your responses by comparing them with Answer Frame 2[19], page 52.

Frame 3[19]

Part B—Long-Term Liabilities (bonds)

Long-term liabilities are those not maturing within the ensuing year or within the operating cycle of the entity (in case the cycle extends beyond the ensuing year). The most common long-term liabilities are bonds and long-term notes payable, usually supported by a mortgage on specific assets. Bonds may be *straight* (ordinary) bonds, which mature all at one time, or *serial* bonds, which mature at a series of stated intervals. *Callable* bonds can be called in and paid off at any time at the option of the borrower. *Convertible* bonds are, at the *investor's* option, convertible into other specified securities of the borrower, typically common stock.

Amortization of Premium and Discount on Bonds Payable. When bonds are sold, any premium or discount should be recorded in a separate account. Amortization procedures are identical with those discussed in Part A for the investor. To illustrate, assume a $10,000, 5% bond issue was sold on April 1, 19A, for $10,280.08. Semiannual interest dates are March 31 and September 30 each year. To simplify the illustration we will assume the bonds have only a three-year life. *Selected* entries over the life of the issue are reviewed below:

a. To record sale of the bonds on April 1, 19A (immediately after an interest date):

Cash	10,280.08	
Premium on bonds payable		280.08
Bonds payable		10,000.00

Alternatively, had the bonds been sold on June 1, 19A, we would have to recognize two months' accrued interest, as follows:

Cash ($10,280.08 + 2 months' accrued interest)	10,363.41	
Interest expense ($10,000 × 5% × 2/12)		83.33
Premium on bonds payable		280.08
Bonds payable		10,000.00

b. To record interest payment on September 30, 19A (and each interest period thereafter). Premium is amortized on a straight-line basis each six months:

Interest expense	203.32	
Premium on bonds payable ($280.08 ÷ 6 semiannual periods) . .	46.68	
Cash ($10,000 × 5% × 6/12)		250.00

c. Entry to redeem the bonds at maturity. (Note that the Premium on bonds payable account now has a zero balance.)

Bonds payable	10,000	
Cash		10,000

Interest Method Amortization of Bond Premium and Discount. At the beginning of Frame 2[19] two methods of amortizing bond premium and discount were listed—the straight-line and the interest methods. The straight-line method has been initially reviewed to illustrate the entries to record amortization of premium and discount. At this point the interest method is reviewed. This method should be used because it is theoretically preferable. However, where the difference between interest method and straight-line method is not material, the straight-line method is acceptable. To illustrate the interest method we utilize the immediately preceding illustration. Reference to a bond table (Illustration 19–1) indicates that a $10,000, 5%, three-year bond with semiannual interest that sold to yield 4% would cost $10,280.08. An *Amortization table* should be constructed to show the premium amortization and the journal entries at each interest period (Illustration 19–4).

In reviewing this method, you should study the development of the amortization table carefully. Note that the amount of interest each period decreases since it involves application of the 4% yield rate to the decreasing carrying value of the bonds payable. Thus, the amount of premium amortized each

Answer frame 2[19]

1. False. The amount of interest income for 1978 is $590.28, which is the nominal, or cash, interest of $500 plus the discount amortization of $90.28 applicable to 1978.
2. True. Investors were induced to pay a premium in order to get the high cash interest on the bonds. The price of $10,280.07 thus reduced the yield rate to the market rate prevailing at the time the bonds were acquired.
3. False. Straight-line depreciation assumes a constant amount of amortization and hence a constant amount of total interest per period. Because the carrying value is changing to reflect the effect of amortization, the rate of interest is changing per period.
4. True. This is necessary because corporations do not split an amount of interest paid in cash for a semiannual (or other) interest period between two (or more) persons, each of whom held its bonds for a partial interest period.

If you missed any of the above, reread Frame 2[19] before proceeding. Then turn to Frame 3[19], page 51, and continue reading.

Frame 3[19] continued

Illustration 19–4

Interest Method Amortization Table for Bonds Payable ($10,000, 3-year, 5%, semiannual, to yield 4%)

Dates	*Cash Cr.* (*a*)	*Bond Interest Expense Dr.* (*b*)	*Premium on Bonds Payable Dr.* (*c*)	*Liability Carrying Value* (*d*)
4/1/77 . . .	—	—	—	$10,280.08
9/30/77 . . .	$ 250	$ 205.60	$ 44.40	10,235.68
3/31/78 . . .	250	204.71	45.29	10,190.39
9/30/78 . . .	250	203.81	46.19	10,144.20
3/31/79 . . .	250	202.88	47.12	10,097.08
9/30/79 . . .	250	201.94	48.06	10,049.02
3/31/80 . . .	250	200.98	49.02	10,000.00
	$1,500	$1,219.92	$280.08	

Sequential computations:
(*a*) $\$10,000 \times 0.05 \times 6/12 = \$250$.
(*b*) $\$10,280.08 \times 0.04 \times 6/12 = \$205.60$.
(*c*) $\$250 - \$205.60 = \$44.40$.
(*d*) $\$10,280.08 - \$44.40 = \$10,235.68$.

period increases—because the cash interest remains constant. Note in particular that the rate of interest remains constant per semiannual period at 2%. This reflects the theoretical preferability of the interest method. It should also be clear that bonds acquired at a discount will produce an increasing amount of interest per period as the rate is held constant and applied to a carrying value that is rising over time toward maturity value (on the maturity date). The same approach (and amounts, in this instance) would apply to the investor's books, assuming the interest method was also used by him.

True or false?

_______ 1. Accounting for long-term bonds payable involves the same dollar amounts as accounting for long-term investments in bonds for the two parties to the transaction in which the bonds are originally issued. Only the account titles differ.

_______ 2. The issuer and the investor can both use the same amortization table in accounting for interest and amortization on long-term bonds.

_______ 3. If two corporations issue identical 10-year bonds at the same premium and Issuer 1 amortizes the premium on the straight-line basis while Issuer 2 amortizes the premium on the interest method, in year 1 of the life of the bonds, Issuer 1 will report the lower interest expense.

_______ 4. Consider the same fact situation given in question 3 above. Over the concurrent life of the two bond issues, Issuer 2 will report the greater interest expense.

Now check your responses by comparing them with Answer Frame 3[19], page 54.

Frame 4[19]

Reporting Bond Discount and Premium on the Balance Sheet. Bond premium and bond discount should be reported on the balance sheet in the following ways:

1. On the *investor's* balance sheet the bond investment should be reported as an asset under the caption "Investments and Funds." Any unamortized bond premium should be added to the par (maturity) value of the bond investment; any unamortized bond discount should be deducted.
2. On the *borrower's* balance sheet the bond liability should be reported under the caption "Long-term Liabilities." Any unamortized bond premium should be added to the maturity value of the bond liability, and any unamortized bond discount deducted.

Convertible Bonds. Convertible bonds provide that under specified conditions, the holder may elect to convert them to other securities of the borrowing corporation. Conversion privilege generally is in terms of common stock. Thus, convertible bonds offer the investor the possibility of capital appreciation through the potential appreciation of the price of the issuing company's stock. As a result, issuers are typically able to assign a lower interest rate on convertible bonds than on similar nonconvertible bonds.

Investors in convertible bonds are purchasing two securities, the bonds and the conversion option. Therefore, in theory, the cash proceeds should be apportioned between Bonds Payable and Contributed Capital from Convertibility of Bonds. However, there typically exists no basis for making the apportionment; therefore, the entire proceeds are credited to the Bonds Payable (plus Premium or less Discount) account. Additional justification for this treatment lies in the fact that the bonds are *not* contributed capital prior to conversion.

The theoretically preferable method of accounting for *the conversion* requires that the market value of the bonds or the other security, whichever is more clearly determinable, be used as a basis for recording the conversion transaction. To illustrate, assume the following account balances on a bond interest date:

Bonds payable, convertible	$100,000
Premium on bonds payable	5,000

A bondholder submits a $1,000 bond for conversion to common stock; the conversion privilege specifies that each $1,000 bond may be converted to eight shares of common stock, par value $100 per share. At the date of the conversion the stock was quoted on the market at $132 per share. The conversion transaction would be recorded as follows:

Bonds payable	1,000	
Premium on bonds payable $5,000 × ($1,000 ÷ $100,000)	50	
Loss on bond conversion (amount required to balance the entry)	6	
Common stock (par value—8 shares × $100)		800
Contributed capital in excess of par—common ($132 − $100) × 8 shares		256

Answer frame 3[19]

1. True. This answer assumes that both the issuer (with *bonds payable*) and the initial investor (with an *investment* in bonds) use the same method of amortizing bond premium or bond discount. If they use different amortization methods, the *periodic* amounts of interest and amortization will differ, but the total amounts will remain the same.
2. True. This answer is related to the answer to question 1 above and also holds *only* when both the issuer and the initial investor use the same method of amortizing premium or discount. Otherwise they will need to use different amortization tables.
3. True. Issuer 2's interest expense in Year 1 will be greater because he is applying the true yield rate to the premium price while Issuer 1 is computing the same amount of interest expense in all ten years. This differential will reverse in Years 6 through 10, with Issuer 1 reporting the greater interest expense in those years. See Illustrations 19–2 and 19–4.
4. False. Total interest expense is the same for both issuers. Only the amounts of interest assigned to specific periods is different for the two methods.

If you missed any of the above questions, reread Frame 3[19] before proceeding. Then turn to Frame 4[19], page 53, and continue reading.

Frame 4[19] continued

In the event that market values are not available, or are not reliable, the conversion entry may be based on the book value of the bonds in which case no gain or loss will be reported inasmuch as the stock is recorded at the book value of the bonds that are being converted.

Serial Bonds. An issue of bonds calling for repayment in a series of installments is called a serial bond issue. For example, a corporation may issue 20-year bonds of $100,000 with the provision that repayment will be $20,000 per year starting at the end of the 16th year. The only unique problem encountered in serial bonds (as compared with straight bonds) is the amortization of any premium or discount. Either the interest or straight-line method may be employed.

Early Extinguishment of Debt. Bonds may be retired prior to maturity. This early extinguishment can occur in a number of ways. For example, the issuing corporation may have an excess of cash and desire to pay off the bonds payable. Another possibility is that the issuer may decide to refund the outstanding bonds payable with a refunding issue, that is, issue new bonds to retire the old bonds. Refunding typically takes place in response to decreases in market interest rates, thus making refunding economically advantageous by reducing interest payments.

The issuer who is contemplating refunding should compare the present value of the outstanding bonds against the cash outlay necessary to retire the old bonds. In many cases, there is a call price, which will constitute the required cash outlay. To illustrate refunding, assume that $100,000 of 8% bonds payable with a book value of $99,000 (i.e., unamortized discount of $1,000) are callable at 101. The market interest rate has fallen to 7%, and the issuer determines that it is desirable to refund the 8% bonds with $101,000 maturity value of 7% bonds. Bond prices have risen dramatically in response to the decline in interest rates, such that the market price (i.e., present value) of the old bonds is 104. Nevertheless, the call feature enables the issuer to call the 8% bonds at 101. The entries to record the refunding are:

a. To issue 7% bonds at par:

Cash	101,000	
Bonds payable, 7%		101,000

b. To retire 8% bonds:

Bonds payable, 8%	100,000	
Extraordinary loss on early extinguishment of bonds payable	2,000	
Discount on bonds payable		1,000
Cash		101,000

APB Opinion No. 26 requires that gains or losses on all early extinguishments be reported on the income statement of the period the extinguishment occurs. FASB *Statement No. 4* requires that such gains and losses be labeled as "Extraordinary."

Is each of the following statements true or false?

_______ 1. Discount on bonds payable should be reported on the borrower's balance sheet as a deferred charge.

_______ 2. When debt securities are converted to other securities, the gain or loss on conversion is computed by comparing the market value of the security canceled with the market value of the security issued.

_______ 3. When a bond payable is due within one year of the current balance sheet date or within the operating cycle (whichever is longer), the bond liability should be reclassified as a current liability.

_______ 4. In general, a firm that refunds bonds payable in order to obtain a more favorable interest rate will report a loss on refunding whereas a firm that refunds at a higher rate will report a gain.

Now check your responses by comparing them with Answer Frame 4[19], page 56.

Answer frame 4[19]

1. False. Discount on bonds payable should be reported on the balance sheet as a deduction from the bond liability.
2. False. When debt securities are converted, the gain or loss is computed by comparing the *book value* of the debt security with the *market value* of the security into which the debt security was converted.
3. True. A bond liability which is due within one year of the balance sheet, or within the operating cycle, it should be reclassified as a current liability. However, if the maturing bond liability will be replaced by another long-term liability, the maturing liability makes no claim on *current* assets and hence should not be reclassified as current.
4. True. As interest rates fall, bond prices rise, and vice versa. Therefore, if a corporation refunds at a higher interest rate (generally an economically unsound decision unless the principal amount of the new bonds is enough less than the old bonds to offset the interest differential), the issuer will be able to repay the old bonds at a market price which will probably be less than the book value of the old bonds and hence result in a gain. The opposite is true of a refunding at a lower interest rate.

If you missed any of the above questions, reread Frame 4[19] before proceeding to Chapter 20.

chapter 20

ACCOUNTING CHANGES, ERROR CORRECTION, AND INCOMPLETE RECORDS

Frame 1[20]

Accounting Changes

Occasionally accounting changes must be made due to changing circumstances. Any time an accounting change is made, there exists the potential for users of financial statements to be unable to make interperiod comparisons. For example, a 19B income statement in which cost of sales includes beginning inventory accounted for on a Fifo basis and ending inventory on a Lifo basis is not directly comparable to a 19B income statement of the same company that used Fifo throughout 19A, unless prices remain constant. Interperiod comparability is a critical conceptual issue in the area of accounting changes.

APB Opinion No. 20 deals with recording and reporting the different types of accounting changes. It identifies three types of accounting changes, as well as error corrections. Illustration 20–1 below

Illustration 20–1

Type of Accounting Change	*Treatment*	*Method of Implementing Change*
1. Reporting entity	Retroactive	Restate on the new basis prior periods' financial statements that are presented in comparative form with statements of the change year.
2. Accounting principle	Current with pro forma restatement of prior periods' statements	Report a catch-up adjustment in the manner similar to an extraordinary item on the income statement of the change year. Report on the new basis in the year of the change. Do not restate prior periods' financial statements. Instead, present as a supplement to the income statement the amount of pro forma net income of prior periods as though the new basis had been in effect in the prior periods (pro forma means "as if").
3. Accounting estimate	Current and prospective	Use the new estimate in conjunction with existing book values to compute amounts using the new basis in the current and future periods. Do not record a catch-up adjustment and do not restate prior period statements.
4. Accounting error*	Current or retroactive	If the error was made in the current period, only the current period financial statements will be affected by the correction. If the error was made in a prior period and was discovered in the current period, determine the under- or overstatement of all affected prior periods' accounts including all prior net incomes. All incorrect account balances must be corrected. If there was a misstatement of net income, the correction should be made as a Prior Period Adjustment, which is closed to the Retained Earnings account.

* Accounting errors are *not* necessarily accounting changes. However, correction of an error may involve an accounting change from an unacceptable method to a method that is generally accepted.

identifies the types of accounting changes, the treatment accorded the various types, and the method of implementing the required treatment. In the column headed Method of Implementing Change it deals with one of the two accounting issues involving accounting changes. The two issues are (1) recording the change and (2) reporting the change, and the illustration speaks directly to the reporting issue.

The discussion that follows defines the various types of accounting changes, lists some examples of each type, illustrates the method of *recording* the change, and also illustrates the method of *reporting* the change in the financial statements. Throughout it is assumed that the company making the change presents two years' financial statements together in comparative form.

1. Change in *reporting entity*. The composition (i.e., the subsidiary companies) of one year's consolidated financial statements is different from the composition of another year's consolidated financial statements of the same parent company. For example, assume that Company A owns two subsidiaries, Company Y and Company Z. In 19A, the three companies are combined in a set of consolidated financial statements, whereas for some appropriate reason, the 19B consolidated financial statements report on Company A and only one of its subsidiaries, Company Y. In this case, the 19A financial statements would be restated retroactively to exclude Company Z for comparative presentation along with the 19B financial statements. In this way, interperiod comparability is achieved. The change in reporting entity is covered in a more advanced accounting course and is not given additional treatment here.

2. Change in *accounting principle*. When a change is made from one method of accounting to another method (as opposed to a change in an estimate), such as a change from straight-line depreciation

to sum-of-the-years'-digits method, there is a change in accounting principle. Other examples are a change from the cost method to the equity method of accounting for long-term investments in stock and a change from capitalization of certain costs to expensing the costs as incurred. For these kinds of changes, *Opinion No. 20* specifies that a *changeover entry* must be made and that a special debit or credit catch-up adjustment must be recorded.

To illustrate the recording of a change in an accounting principle, assume that a company has been depreciating a machine on the straight-line method for two years. Effective at the beginning of Year 3, the firm decides to change to the double-declining-balance method. The machine cost $20,000, has a ten-year life and no estimated residual value. The entry to record the accounting change would be:

Adjustment—due to accounting change			3,200	
Accumulated depreciation				3,200
Computations:				
Straight-line depreciation (old method):				
$20,000 × 1/10 × 2		$4,000		
Double-declining-balance depreciation (new method):				
Year 1: $20,000 × 20%	$4,000			
Year 2: ($20,000 − $4,000) × 20%	3,200	7,200		
Addition accumulated depreciation to be recorded		$3,200		

To illustrate the reporting of this change in accounting principle, assume that income before extraordinary items was $10,000 for Year 2 and $11,000 for Year 3. Selected portions of the Year 3 and Year 2 comparative financial statements are as follows (ignoring income taxes and omitting per share data):

	Year 2	*Year 3*
Balance Sheet		
Accumulated depreciation	$ 4,000	$ 9,760
Computations:		
Year 2: $4,000 (from above)		
Year 3: $4,000 (year 2) + $3,200 (changeover entry) + [($20,000 − $7,200) × 20%] = $9,760		
Income Statement:		
Depreciation expense	$ 2,000	
($20,000 − $7,200) × 20%		$ 2,560
Income before extraordinary items	10,000	11,000
Adjustment due to change in accounting principle		(3,200)
Net Income	10,000	7,800
Pro forma net income, reflecting retroactive application of accounting change*	$ 8,800	$11,000

*Computations:
Year 2: $10,000 − $3,200 (double-declining-balance depreciation for year 2) × $2,000 (add back year 2 straight-line depreciation) = $8,800.
Year 3: $7,800 + $3,200 (add back changeover adjustment, which would not have been made if double-declining-balance depreciation had been used from inception) = $11,000.

As an exception to the general rule, *APB Opinion No. 20* requires that some changes in accounting principle (generally those that cause credit adjustment) be given retroactive effect in the accounts by restating prior years' financial statements on the new basis. These types of changes are (1) any change from Lifo to another cost flow method for inventory, (2) a change in the method of accounting for revenue on long-term construction contracts, and (3) a change to or from the full cost method of accounting for expenses in an extractive minerals industry.

3. Change in *accounting estimate.* The use of estimates, such as in accounting for depreciation and bad debts, is a natural consequence of the accounting process. From time to time, experience and additional information suggest that prior estimates still being used should be changed. For example, a fixed asset has been depreciated on the basis of a 10-year life; shortly after the end of the 6th year it is de-

cided that the total useful life is more realistically estimated to be 15 years. Changes of this type are known as changes in *estimate* as opposed to the other types of accounting changes. The *Opinion* states that when there is a change in estimate, no catch-up adjustment should be made; rather the remaining (undepreciated) balance should be apportioned over the remaining useful life. To illustrate, assume that the above asset originally cost $22,500. With no residual value and assuming straight-line depreciation, for each of the first six years the following depreciation entry would have been made:

Depreciation expense	2,250	
Accumulated depreciation		2,250

With the change in accounting estimate, the entry for the 7th and each succeeding year (through Year 15) would be:

Depreciation expense	1,000	
Accumulated depreciation		1,000

Computations:

Original cost	$22,500
Depreciation to date of change ($22,500 × 6/10)	13,500
To be depreciated over remaining life	$ 9,000

Annual depreciation under new estimate: $9,000 ÷ 9 years = $1,000

Thus, the comparative income statements for Year 7 and Year 6 will report Depreciation Expense of $1,000 and $2,250, respectively. The amounts of Accumulated Depreciation on the comparative balance sheets of Year 7 and Year 6 would be $14,500 and $13,500, respectively.

4. Change due to *error*. This deals with outright errors as opposed to changes in estimates for sound reasons and changes in accounting principles. Errors usually involve outright omissions such as failing to record depreciation for the year or recording an incorrect amount. Clearly, when an error is found in the accounts, it should be corrected. If the error was made during the current year, a simple correction entry is necessary since account balances for prior years are unaffected. To illustrate, assume that a fixed asset costing $2,000 was purchased during February of the current year (before the books are closed) and that it was incorrectly debited to the purchases account. The correcting entry would be:

Fixed assets (identified)	2,000	
Purchases		2,000

In contrast, an error that was made in a prior period and has never been corrected may be discovered. This situation presents a slightly more complex adjusting entry. *APB Opinion No. 20* specifies that the net effect of the adjustment of prior period balances must be recorded as a Prior Period Adjustment which is closed to Retained Earnings. To illustrate, assume that a fixed asset costing $5,000 was purchased January 19A; however, at that time the cost was incorrectly debited to purchases. It is now at the end of 19B, and the error has just been discovered. Obviously, no depreciation has been taken for Years 19A and 19B; however, the books for 19B have not yet been closed. Assuming a ten-year useful life and no residual value, the correction entry would be:

Fixed asset (identified)	5,000	
Depreciation expense (for 19B)	500	
Accumulated depreciation (2 years)		1,000
Prior period adjustment—correction of error		4,500

You should observe that the reported net income for 19A was understated by $4,500 ($5,000 – $500); this entry serves to correct retained earnings (through the Prior Period Adjustment account) for that error.

Procedures for Correcting Errors

When errors are found in financial statements and/or accounting records, they should be carefully analyzed. Analysis and correction involves the following three steps:

1. Identify the error and its precise effect.
2. Determine how the transaction or item should have been recorded.
3. Determine the best way to make the correction.

Some errors affect only the balance sheet; others affect only the income statement; and still others affect both statements. In the analysis and correction of errors it is useful to classify them as:

1. Noncounterbalancing errors, that is, errors that continue to affect account balances (hence financial statements) until corrected. Examples are misstatement of the depreciation charge and recording a capital expenditure as an expense.
2. Counterbalancing errors, that is, errors that at the end of *two* consecutive periods will counterbalance. The financial statements for both periods will be in error by the same amounts, but in the opposite directions. Examples of counterbalancing errors are:
   a. Errors in inventory—this type of error is counterbalancing because the final inventory for one period is the beginning inventory for the next period and they have *opposite* effects on income. To illustrate, assume the final inventory for 19A is *understated* by $1,000; the effect is:
   19A income statement—Ending inventory understated.
   —Cost of goods sold overstated.
   —Income understated.
   19A balance sheet —Assets (inventory) understated.
   —Retained earnings understated.
   19B income statement—Beginning inventory understated.
   —Cost of goods sold understated.
   —Income overstated.
   19B balance sheet —No misstatements.
   b. Errors in adjusting for accrued and deferred items, since these items have a "carry-over effect" similar to inventory. To illustrate, assume accrued wages of $500 were not recognized in 19A (an entry should have been made debiting Wage Expense for $500 and crediting Wages Payable for $500); the effect of the omission is:
   19A income statement—Wage expense understated.
   —Income overstated.
   19A balance sheet —Current liabilities understated.
   —Retained earnings overstated.
   19B income statement—Wage expense overstated.
   —Income understated.
   19B balance sheet —No misstatement.

Another important factor in the analysis and correction of errors is to determine the status of the accounts, that is, whether or not the books have been *adjusted and closed.* The correcting entry required generally will be affected by this factor. To illustrate two typical situations:

Situation 1—Noncounterbalancing error. Assume an asset that cost $10,000 was acquired on January 1, 19A. The asset was depreciated at 15% per year in 19A, whereas the rate should have been 10% per year. The error was discovered at the end of 19B:

a. Before the books were adjusted and closed for 19B; therefore, the correcting entry would be:

Accumulated depreciation ($1,500 – $1,000, all for 19A)	500	
Prior Period Adjustment—depreciation correction		500

b. After the books were adjusted and closed for 19B; therefore, the correcting entry would be:

Accumulated depreciation ($3,000 – $2,000)	1,000	
Prior Period Adjustment—depreciation correction		1,000

Situation 2—Counterbalancing error. Assume that a $2,000 purchase in 19A was not recorded until 19B; the goods represented by the purchase also were not included in the 19A inventory (that is, two errors were made). The error was discovered in 19B after the related payment was made and—

a. Before the books were closed for 19B; therefore, the correcting entry would be:

Beginning inventory	2,000	
Purchases (19B)		2,000

(Note: Since the item was omitted from both purchases and inventory in 19A, the 19A reported income was correct—they offset. However, on the 19A balance sheet, inventory and accounts payable each were understated by $2,000.)

b. After the books were adjusted and closed for 19B; therefore, the correcting entry would be:

Counterbalanced in 19B—no correcting entry required.

True or false?

_______ 1. The accounting for accounting changes and error corrections generally involves comparing prior periods' amounts that were reported earlier, to amounts for the prior periods that would have been reported if the company had used the new basis in the prior periods.

_______ 2. Accounting errors are a special type of accounting change.

_______ 3. The catch-up adjustment in the income statement is used only for changes in accounting principle.

_______ 4. Pro forma presentation is used only for changes in accounting principles.

Now check your responses by comparing them with Answer Frame 1[20], page 62.

Frame 2[20]

Single-Entry and Incomplete Records

Ideally a business, whether large or small, maintains a reasonably complete set of accounting records based on (*a*) the double-entry concept and (*b*) the accounting equation (Assets = Liabilities + Owners' Equity). However, it is not unusual to encounter small businesses that maintain only the "bare essentials"; that is, they have incomplete records and single-entry records. Yet, it is frequently necessary to prepare financial statements from the incomplete records. The paragraphs to follow review the basic procedures that have been found useful in such situations.

Balance Sheet Prepared from Incomplete Records

The first step is to gather all of the records that have been maintained, such as the check stubs, deposit slips, charge sales tickets, income tax returns, prior financial statements, bank statements, and insurance policies. In constructing a balance sheet from incomplete records, the assets must be inventoried and valued at approximate cost, then the accumulated depreciation estimated. Liabilities must be listed from such sources as correspondence with creditors and discussions with the owners. Of course, the net of these two major balance sheet categories provides the amount of owners' equity. To illustrate, assume your investigation revealed the following information in respect to the business conducted by A. A. Brown. From these data you are to prepare a balance sheet.

The bank statement balance plus cash on hand amounted to $2,345. An inventory of merchandise, priced at replacement cost, amounted to $1,550. Inspection of miscellaneous records revealed that the

Answer frame 1[20]

1. False. The statement is true for changes in reporting entities, changes in accounting principles, and error corrections. It is not true for changes in accounting estimates.
2. False. Errors are not accounting changes. But because both errors and changes frequently involve amounts that have already been recorded in the accounts, it is convenient to discuss them in the same context.
3. True. The catch-up adjustment is not used for changes in reporting entities or for changes in accounting estimates.
4. True. The pro forma presentation presents the current and prior periods' net income before extraordinary items and net income that would have been reported if the company had used the newly adopted accounting principle in both accounting periods. The pro forma presentation is not used for changes in reporting entities nor for changes in accounting estimates.

If you missed any of the above questions, reread Frame 1[20] before proceeding. Then go to Frame 2[20], page 61, and continue reading.

Frame 2[20] continued

company had acquired store and office equipment on January 1 costing $500. A reasonable rate of depreciation of this asset was estimated to be 5% per annum. A short-term note for $50 signed by a customer was on hand. In addition the "charge" book showed that four customers owed bills amounting to $90. From the cashbook it was determined that Brown had purchased supplies costing $15 during the period. Since no supplies were on hand, it must be assumed that they were used during the period. There were no liabilities except for two accounts payable (from an "accounts payable" file) amounting to $240.

The resulting balance sheet is shown in Illustration 20–1; owners' equity was determined by subtracting total liabilities from total assets.

Illustration 20–1

A. A. BROWN
Balance Sheet, December 31, 19A

Assets			
Current Assets:			
Cash		$2,345	
Notes receivable		50	
Accounts receivable:			
A. B. Cottle	$25		
R. S. Thomas	30		
N. O. Page	10		
B. C. Davis	25	90	
Merchandise inventory		1,550	
Total Current Assets			$4,035
Fixed Assets:			
Office and store fixtures (depreciated cost)			475
Total Assets			$4,510
Current Liabilities			
Accounts Payable:			
Lee and Jackson		90	
Mason Company		150	
Total Current Liabilities			240
Owners' Equity			
A. A. Brown, proprietorship			$4,270
			$4,510

Net Income Determined from Incomplete Records

Net income may be determined from incomplete records utilizing either of two approaches. The approach to be used depends upon the data available and the amount of detail required. The two methods are:

1. *Shortcut, no detail needed.* The method followed here is to analyze the *difference* between the *beginning* and *ending* owners' equity of the entity. The following generalized equation is utilized:

Net income = Ending owners' equity − Beginning owners' equity + Withdrawals (dividends) − Additional investments (during the period).

Two examples of the application of this formula are shown in Illustration 20–2.

Illustration 20–2

	Computation Where There Has Been	
	A Net Income	*A Net Loss*
Present owners' equity (end of period)	$8,000	$5,500
Prior owners' equity (beginning of period)	7,100	6,300
Change, increase	900	
(decrease)		(800)
Add: Withdrawals	1,200	1,000
	2,100	200
Deduct: Additional investments	500	400
Income for Period	$1,600	
Loss of Period		$(200)

2. *Detailed analysis, detailed statement needed.* Under this approach, each significant item to be reported on the income statement must be analyzed and its amount computed; invoices, bills, cancelled checks, bank statements, and so on, must be analyzed to determine sales, cost of goods sold, and expenses. To illustrate this type of analysis, we have selected *sales.* This approach for sales involves an analysis of *cash receipts* and *accounts receivable.* With respect to cash receipts, let's assume that cash register tapes have been maintained and from them we determine that *cash sales* for the period amounted to $82,400. We find the following information with respect to accounts receivable (no such account has been maintained in the records):

a. Accounts receivable, beginning of period (from a list found in the files that had been prepared at the end of the last year for tax purposes)	$35,000
b. Collections on charge sales during the period (taken from the memoranda prepared with the deposit slips)	42,000
c. Collections on charge sales during period, such collections not deposited (comparison of deposit slips with cash register tapes)	50
d. Accounts receivable, end of period (determined by analysis of charge tickets less cash collections as revealed by deposit slips and cash register tapes)	48,000

Based on these data, sales revenue for the period may be computed as follows:

Accounts receivable, end of period		$ 48,000
Cash collected from customers—deposited	$42,000	
—not deposited	50	42,050
		90,050
Less: Accounts receivable, beginning of period		35,000
Credit sales for the period		55,050
Add: Cash sales for the period		82,400
Total Sales Revenue for the Period		$137,450

Indicate whether each of the following statements is true or false by writing *T* or *F* in the space provided.

______ 1. A set of books maintained under the single-entry concept will not provide the data necessary to prepare the financial statements.

______ 2. If the beginning and ending balances of accounts receivable are $1,000 and $1,800, respectively, and if collections on accounts receivable for the period were $4,000, cash sales must have been $4,800.

______ 3. If the balance sheet shows more total liabilities than total assets, the income statement for the period will report a loss.

______ 4. When net income is computed by comparing beginning and ending owners' equity balances, the declaration of a stock dividend during the period would have no effect on the computations.

Now check your responses by comparing them with Answer Frame 2[20], page 66.

Frame 3[20]

Analysis of Accounts

The analysis of incomplete data frequently may be somewhat complex; as a consequence, students frequently find it helpful to *reconstruct* one or more T-accounts in certain situations. To illustrate, assume your analysis has determined the following with respect to a significant item of expense:

	Beginning Balance	*Ending Balance*
Prepaid expense balance	$700	$900
Accrued expense, i.e., liability balance	300	800
Cash paid on the expense during the period, $7,000.		

You are required to determine the amount of this expense that should be reported on the income statement. This can be done by analysis of the relevant T-accounts.

Prepaid Expense

Debit		Credit	
Beg. bal.	700	(*a*) Expense entry .	700
(*c*) Prepayment entry	900		

Accrued Expense

Debit		Credit	
(*b*) Payment entry	300	Beg. bal.	300
		(*d*) Expense entry .	800

Expense

Debit		Credit	
Paid in cash	7,000		
(*a*) Expense entry—prepaid	700	(*b*) Payment entry—accrued	300
(*d*) Expense entry—accrued	800	(*c*) Prepayment entry—prepaid	900

(Expense for the period to be reported on the income statement—balance in Expense account, $7,300.)

Alternatively, some may prefer the following shortcut method:

Amount of expense paid in cash	$7,000
Net increase in prepaid expense ($900 − $700) . . .	(200)
Net increase in accrued expense ($800 − $300) . . .	500
Expense for the period	$7,300

Note that the analysis in both the above approaches proceeds from the initial assumption that the entire $7,000 paid during the period was for expense. The adjustments are needed because some of the cash payments were for assets (prepaid expense) and some were for liabilities (payment of the beginning accrued expense balance) that *had been expensed* in a prior accounting period.

Worksheet Approach for Incomplete Data Problems

For incomplete data problems a worksheet approach, in most cases, is clearly superior because it provides an organized approach for marshaling the known information and tying the parts together. To illustrate, assume that you are to prepare financial statements for the Masters Company for the year ended December 31, 19A. You have been able to develop the following information:

	Balances	
	January 1	*December 31*
Debits		
Cash	$12,000	$16,000
Accounts receivable (net)	70,000	62,000
Inventories (by count)	30,000	34,000
Prepaid expenses	300	200
Furniture and equipment (net)	34,000	35,000
Credits		
Accounts payable	35,000	30,000
Notes payable		10,000
Accrued expense liability	700	1,000

A. Canceled checks summarized: accounts payable, $62,000; expenses, $31,500; equipment purchases, $4,500.
B. Withdrawals of cash by owner, $300 per week.
C. Bank loan obtained October 1, $10,000, 6% per year, 6 months, deducted in advance.
D. Sold equipment for cash, $1,500, that had a book value of $1,000.
E. Estimated bad debts (based on current sales), $2,000.
F. Sales for the year, $99,000 (small amounts of "miscellaneous revenue" not included).

To organize these data and to develop detail for the income statement and balance sheet you decided to utilize a *worksheet approach*. Although numerous variations of the worksheet are possible, the one shown in Illustration 20–3 is typical. You can use it to prepare the financial statements (and as a basis for starting a *complete double-entry* accounting system for the company). The steps in completing the worksheet are:

1. Enter the *balances given* for assets and liabilities in the *first* and *last* columns; plug the amount for owner's equity.
2. Make the normal journal entries in the Interim Entries, Debit and Credit columns for all the remaining information available. These entries have been keyed on the worksheet with capital letters as *A* through *F*. (They should be studied carefully at this point by the reader.)
3. Make additional journal entries to *account for all of the unexplained differences* between the beginning and ending balances on each line of the worksheet. These entries should proceed from the obvious to the less obvious ones. This group of entries on the illustrative worksheet have been keyed with *lowercase letters* as *g* through *o*. The reader should analyze these entries carefully to ascertain how they were developed. They may be reviewed as follows:
   g. Cash collections from sales recorded as the "plug" figure for accounts receivable as follows:

Debits in the account ($70,000 + $99,000)		$169,000
Credits in the account	$ 2,000	
Ending balance as given	62,000	64,000
Difference—entry due to cash from sales		$105,000

Indicated entry:

Cash	105,000	
Accounts receivable		105,000

Answer frame 2[20]

1. False. Generally it is possible to prepare financial statements using single-entry records; however, special analyses often are required.
2. False. The information given provides no basis for concluding as to the amount of cash sales. It does, however, provide a basis for concluding that sales on account must have been $4,800.
3. False. The information given indicates a deficit in owners' equity; however, this does not indicate when the deficit was incurred nor the causes of the deficit.
4. True. Since net income is being computed on total owners' equity and not just on retained earnings, a stock dividend would not affect the computation.

If you missed any of the above questions, reread Frame 2[20] before proceeding. Then turn to Frame 3[20], page 64, and continue reading.

Frame 3[20] continued

Illustration 20–3

MASTERS COMPANY
Incomplete Records: Worksheet for Year Ending December 31, 19A

	Beginning Balances January 1, 19A	Interim Entries		Income Statement	Ending Balances December 31, 19A
		Debit	Credit		
Debit accounts:					
Cash	12,000	(*C*) 9,700	(*A*) 98,000		16,000
		(*D*) 1,500	(*B*) 15,600		
		(*g*) 105,000			
		(*n*) 1,400			
Accounts receivable (net)	70,000	(*F*) 99,000	(*E*) 2,000		62,000
			(*g*) 105,000		
Inventories	30,000	(*h*) 4,000			34,000
Prepaid expenses	300	(*i*) 150	(*k*) 250		200
Furniture and equipment (net)	34,000	(*A*) 4,500	(*D*) 1,000		35,000
			(*j*) 2,500		
Expenses		(*A*) 31,500			
		(*k*) 250			
		(*l*) 300		32,050	
Interest expenses		(*C*) 300	(*i*) 150	150	
Depreciation		(*j*) 2,500		2,500	
Purchases		(*m*) 57,000		57,000	
Bad debt expense		(*E*) 2,000		2,000	
Net income (to owner's equity)		(*o*) 11,200		11,200	
	146,300			104,900	147,200
Credit accounts:					
Accounts payable	35,000	(*A*) 62,000	(*m*) 57,000		30,000
Notes payable			(*C*) 10,000		10,000
Accrued expenses	700		(*l*) 300		1,000
Masters, owner's equity	110,600	(*B*) 15,600	(*o*) 11,200		106,200
Sales revenue			(*F*) 99,000	99,000	
Miscellaneous revenue			(*n*) 1,400	1,400	
Inventory change			(*h*) 4,000	4,000	
Gain on sale of fixed assets			(*D*) 500	500	
	146,300	407,900	407,900	104,900	147,200

h. To record the $4,000 increase in inventory.
i. To record the prepaid interest expense on the bank note ($10,000 × 6% × 3/12 = $150).
j. To record the indicated depreciation expense (the "plug" amount necessary to attain the given ending Furniture and equipment account balance is $2,500).
k. To record the credit to prepaid expenses ($250) required to attain the ending balance as given.
l. To record the indicated change in accrued expenses ($1,000 – $700).
m. To record purchases as the amount required to attain the ending balance in accounts payable (computed in the way indicated above for *g*).
n. To record the amount required to "make the Cash account come out"; it is assumed that the $1,400 debit required was derived from "miscellaneous revenue," since this source was indicated but no amount had been accorded it.
o. To record the pretax net income as computed in the Income Statement column.

4. Extend the *net balance* of each revenue and expense line of the worksheet to the Income Statement column; the difference between the credits and debits will be the pretax net income (or loss). Do the same for the balance sheet accounts. Total debits should equal total credits.
5. Check each line on the worksheet for accuracy, including reconciliation of the beginning and ending balance sheet accounts.
6. Column totals on the worksheet should be determined as a good test on accuracy.
7. From the worksheet prepare the formal income statement and balance sheet (not illustrated).

Determine whether each of the following statements is true or false.

_______ 1. Since we prepare financial statements on the accrual basis, knowledge of the cash disbursements related to an expense account tells us nothing about the amount of expense based on the accrual concept.

_______ 2. The T-account approach for the solution of incomplete data problems is an application of algebra.

_______ 3. Refer to the tabulation of accounts and balances near the top of page 65. Disregard the data items A–F beneath the account balances. If cost of goods sold for the year was $70,000, inventory purchases must have been $74,000.

_______ 4. The only transactions that affected accounts receivable during the year were collections on account, sales on account, and a write-off of some individual customers' accounts deemed uncollectible. The algebraic expression of the ending balance is: Beginning balance + Sales – Collections – Write-offs = Ending balance.

Now check your answers by comparing them with Answer Frame 3[20], page 68.

Answer frame 3[20]

1. False. The cash disbursements for a particular expense can be adjusted to the amount of that expense on the accrual basis by considering the changes in any asset (prepaid expense) or liability (accrued expense) account associated with the expense.
2. True. The T-account approach is equivalent to an algebraic equation given by: Beginning balance + Additions − Deductions = Ending balance.
3. True. If Cost of sales = Beginning inventory + Purchases − Ending inventory, then Purchases = Cost of sales − Beginning inventory + Ending inventory, or Purchases = $70,000 − $30,000 + $34,000 = $74,000.
4. True. The expression for the ending balance is an application of the equation given in the answer to Question 2 above. In this application, the reduction in the Accounts Receivable account for uncollectibles is handled correctly as a reduction in the account balance.

If you missed any of the above, reread Frame 3[20] before proceeding. You have now completed Chapter 20. Continue by reading Chapter 21.

chapter 21

STATEMENT OF CHANGES IN FINANCIAL POSITION—WORKING CAPITAL AND CASH

Frame 1[21]

Nature of the Statement of Changes in Financial Position

For many years the accounting profession has required, as a minimum, the presentation of an income statement and a balance sheet. In March 1971, the APB in *Opinion No. 19,* entitled "Reporting Changes in Financial Position" for the first time made a *statement of changes in financial position* mandatory. *APB Opinion No. 19* prescribes the guidelines that should be followed in presenting the information. The statement of changes in financial position may be developed either on (*a*) a working capital basis or (*b*) a cash basis; however, in either approach it must encompass "all financial resources." This latter phrase means that all financing and investing activities must be reported whether or not cash or working capital was involved. For example, the direct exchange of capital stock of the company for a fixed asset, say a plant site, would not involve the inflow or outflow of either cash or working capital. Nevertheless, the transaction must be reported on the statement of changes in financial position.

The balance sheet purports to report on *financial position* at a given point in time. The income statement explains the reasons for the changes in financial position between the beginning and ending balance sheets for a company due to operations. However, there are many changes between the two balance sheets that the income statement does not explain. Specifically, the income statement does not explain those changes caused by a number of *investing* and *financing* activities of the entity during the period. The statement of changes in financial position has this as its objective inasmuch as it reports all of the investing activities (i.e., the cash and working capital outflows for other resources), all of the financing activities (i.e., the cash and working capital inflows from financing transactions), and all other financing and investing activities not directly affecting cash or working capital.

In order to delineate carefully the distinction between a statement of changes in financial position on a working capital basis and on a cash basis, each will be explained separately.

Statement of Changes in Financial Position, Working Capital Basis

Recall that working capital is comprised of current assets and current liabilities and that the *amount* of working capital is current assets minus current liabilities. In preparing a statement of changes in financial position, working capital basis, three categories of data must be identified for the period: (1) inflows (sources) of working capital, (2) outflows (uses) of working capital, and (3) the financing and investing activities that did not affect working capital.

Primary sources (inflows) of working capital:

a. Profits of the business—the revenues of a business less the expenses (except for any noncash expenses such as depreciation) provide an inflow of current assets.
b. Sale of capital stock.
c. Sale of noncurrent assets.
d. Increase in noncurrent liabilities.

Primary uses (outflows) or applications of working capital:

a. Purchase of noncurrent assets such as fixed assets.
b. Purchase of long-term investments.
c. Payment of cash dividends or other similar distributions to owners.
d. Payment of noncurrent liabilities.

Other financing and investing activities (examples):

a. Direct exchange of the firm's own capital stock for a noncurrent asset.
b. Direct exchange of the firm's own stock to extinguish a noncurrent liability.
c. Direct issuance of a noncurrent liability, such as a bond payable, for a noncurrent asset or to extinguish another long-term liability.
d. Trading of one asset for another asset with no cash difference paid or received.

A statement of changes in financial position, working capital basis, is *required* by *Opinion No. 19* to report two separate parts; viz:

Part I —Sources (inflows) of working capital and uses (outflows) of working capital.
Part II—Changes in the working capital accounts.

A statement of changes in financial position, working capital basis, for RT Corporation is presented in Illustration 21–1.

The statement of changes in financial position is relatively easy to understand. In fact, Part II of the statement is simply a comparative statement of the current assets and liabilities that can be taken directly from an adjusted trial balance or from the completed balance sheet. Because of its simplicity it is desirable to prepare Part II initially; this provides a check figure, the amount of increase or decrease in working capital during the period ($10,500 increase in the example) that Part I of the statement is, in part at least, designed to explain. The *development* of Part I, however, is somewhat complex. Due to the

Illustration 21-1

RT CORPORATION
Statement of Changes in Financial Position, Working Capital Basis
For the Year Ended December 31, 19B

Part I—Sources and Uses of Working Capital

Sources of Working Capital		
From operations:		
Net income	$ 8,000	
Adjustments for items included in income but not affecting working capital:		
Depreciation on plant	4,000	
Depreciation on equipment	2,000	
Amortization of patents	500	
Loss on sale of equipment	1,000	
Working Capital Generated from Operations		$15,500
From other sources:		
Sale of equipment	3,000	
Sale of capital stock	10.000	
Total Working Capital from Other Sources		13,000
Other financing activities		
Stock issued for land		5,000
Total Working Capital and Other Resources Generated		33,500
Uses of Working Capital		
Purchase warehouse	3,000	
Payment on long-term notes payable	6,000	
Purchase equipment	9,000	
Other investing activities		
Acquired land (issued capital stock)	5.000	
Total Working Capital and Other Resources Used		23,000
Net Increase in Working Capital during the Year		$10,500

Part II—Changes in Working Capital Accounts

	Balances December 31		Working Capital Increase (Decrease)
	19B	*19A*	
Current Assets:			
Cash	$12,500	$ 5,000	$ 7,500
Accounts receivable (net)	10,000	7,000	3,000
Inventory	8,000	9,000	(1,000)
Total Current Assets	$30,500	$21,000	
Current Liabilities:			
Accounts payable	$ 7,000	$ 6,000	(1,000)
Accrued wages		2.000	2,000
Total Current Liabilities	7,000	8,000	
Working Capital	$23.500	$13,000	$10,500*

* Increase during the period per above.

complexity and volume of data that must be analyzed, a *worksheet* is necessary except for the simplest of situations.

Indicate whether each of the following statements is true or false by writing *T* or *F* in the space provided.

_______ 1. Inclusion of the statement of changes in financial position in the annual report (with the income statement and balance sheet) is optional.

_______ 2. Transactions that do not affect cash or working capital are not included in the statement of changes in financial position as sources or applications.

_______ 3. The statement of changes in financial position, working capital basis, includes two *unrelated* parts.

_______ 4. Illustration 21–1 reported no transactions that did not directly affect working capital.

Now check your responses by comparing them with Answer Frame 1[21], page 72.

Frame 2[21]

Worksheet to Develop Statement of Changes in Financial Position, Working Capital Basis

You have examined the statement of changes in financial position; now let's consider the analytical procedures essential to its development. To illustrate its development, assume that the following data were available with respect to the RT Corporation for the year ended December 31, 19B:

1. RT Corporation post-closing trial balance:

	December 31	
Debits	*19A*	*19B*
Cash	$ 5,000	$ 12,500
Accounts receivable (net)	7,000	10,000
Inventory	9,000	8,000
Long-term investments	3,000	3,000
Plant	30,000	30,000
Equipment	20,000	21,000
Warehouse		11,000
Patents	7,000	6,500
Land—plant site	10,000	15,000
	$91,000	$117,000
Credits		
Accumulated depreciation—plant	$ 6,000	$ 10,000
Accumulated depreciation—equipment	10,000	8,000
Accounts payable	6,000	7,000
Accrued wages payable	2,000	
Long-term notes payable	12,000	14,000
Capital stock (par $10)	50,000	65,000
Retained earnings	5,000	13,000
	$91,000	$117,000

2. Additional data relating to operations and the financing and investing activities:

a. Net income for the year, $8,000.
b. Depreciation on plant for the year, $4,000.
c. Depreciation on equipment for the year, $2,000.
d. Amortization of patents for the year, $500.
e. At the end of the year sold equipment costing $8,000 (50% depreciated) for $3,000 cash; the gain or loss was recorded in the Income Summary account.
f. Purchased warehouse costing $11,000 paid $3,000 cash, gave long-term note for the balance.
g. Paid $6,000 on long-term notes.
h. Sold $10,000 capital stock at par.
i. Purchased equipment costing $9,000 paid one-half cash, balance due in 12 months.
j. Issued 500 shares of stock for additional land for future plant site.

Answer frame 1[21]

1. False. *APB Opinion No. 19* makes this financial statement mandatory.
2. False. *APB Opinion No. 19* requires the "all financial resources" approach regardless of whether working capital or cash is directly affected. For example, if a transaction involves the exchange of bonds for a building (two noncurrent accounts, Bonds Payable and Buildings are affected), the transaction must be included as a source and an application.
3. False. The net sources and uses in working capital are reported in Part I as the investing and financing activities. But Part II reports only the change in the current accounts.
4. False. Capital stock was issued for land. This exchange was listed both as a source (issuance of stock) and a use (acquisition of land). Inclusion of this item is required under the "all financial resources" concept. It was "valued" at $5,000 which represents the fair market value of either the land or the stock (whichever is the most clearly determinable).

If you missed any of the above, you should restudy Frame 1[21] before turning to Frame 2[21], page 71.

Frame 2[21] continued

Starting with the above data for RT Corporation we may proceed to develop the worksheet as follows:

a. Develop Part II of the statement of changes in financial position simply by selecting the current assets and current liabilities from the two post-closing trial balances and computing the change for each item as in Illustration 21–1. Thus, this part is prepared without any specific analytical work once the trial balance data are at hand.

b. Prepare a *worksheet* to analyze sources and uses of working capital as shown in Illustration 21–2. The steps in developing this worksheet analysis are:

Step 1. Lay out the worksheet with the *four* amount columns and the *four* major side captions; with respect to the latter, leave sufficient space for the apparent needs of the problem.

Step 2. Enter the trial balances in the first and last columns; show the working capital net, and the noncurrent items account by account.

Step 3. Enter on the worksheet under the Interim Entries columns all entries during the period that *affected the noncurrent accounts;* the *causes* of the increases and decreases in working capital will be found by analyzing the noncurrent accounts. Do not record entries that affected *only* working capital accounts. The entries are made on the worksheet (as to debits and credits) precisely as they were in the accounts except that *debits and credits* to working capital accounts are entered under the appropriate sections set up at the bottom of the worksheet. It turns out that such debits are "working capital provided" and the credits are "working capital applied." The entries on the worksheet are based upon the "additional data" given, which represent *all* entries for the period that affected noncurrent accounts. The entries on the worksheet should be studied carefully; they may be explained as follows:[1]

Entry (*a*)—The net income in the accounts for the year was debited to Income Summary (closing entry) and credited to Retained Earnings; it *provided funds,* hence, the worksheet entry is:

Working capital provided (net income)	8,000	
Retained earnings		8,000

Entry (*b*)—The depreciation on plant was recorded in the books as a debit to Depreciation Expense and a credit to Accumulated Depreciation. Depreciation is a noncash expense on the income statement

[1] Numerous worksheets have been developed for this analysis; the one illustrated here has proven to be the easiest to understand and provides the essential flexibility to handle the most complex problems in minimum time.

(no cash disbursement involved); hence, it should be added back to profits (working capital provided). This is because beginning with net income as a source of working capital implicitly assumes that all revenues increase working capital and that all expenses decrease working capital. As a result of this assumption, any revenues (expenses) that do not increase (decrease) working capital will provide the need for an adjustment to the net income amount in arriving at working capital provided by operations. The entry on the worksheet then is:

Working capital provided—adjustment to net income (depreciation) . . .	4,000	
Accumulated depreciation		4,000

Entry (*c*)—Depreciation on equipment—same explanation as (*b*):

Working capital provided—adjustment to net income (depreciation) . . .	2,000	
Accumulated depreciation		2,000

Illustration 21–2

	Balances December 31, 19A	Analysis of Interim Entries		Balances December 31, 19B
		Debit	Credit	
Debits				
Working capital (net)	13,000	(*k*) 10,500		23,500
Noncurrent accounts:				
Long-term investments	3,000			3,000
Plant	30,000			30,000
Equipment	20,000	(*i*) 9,000	(*e*) 8,000	21,000
Warehouse		(*f*) 11,000		11,000
Patents	7,000		(*d*) 500	6,500
Land—plant site	10.000	(*j*) 5,000		15,000
	83,000			110,000
Credits				
Accumulated depreciation—plant	6,000		(*b*) 4,000	10,000
Accumulated depreciation—equipment	10,000	(*e*) 4,000	(*c*) 2,000	8,000
Long-term notes payable	12,000	(*g*) 6,000	(*f*) 8,000	14,000
Capital stock (par $10)	50,000		(*h*) 10,000	65,000
			(*j*) 5,000	
Retained earnings	5.000		(*a*) 8,000	13,000
	83.000	45,500	45.500	110,000
Working Capital Provided By:				
Operations:				
Net income		(*a*) 8,000		
Adjustments for changes to income not affecting working capital:				
Depreciation on plant		(*b*) 4,000		
Depreciation on equipment		(*c*) 2,000		
Amortization of patents		(*d*) 500		
Loss on sale of equipment		(*e*) 1,000		
Other sources:				
Sale of equipment		(*e*) 3,000		
Sale of capital stock		(*h*) 10,000		
Other financing activities:				
Issued stock for land		(*j*) 5,000		
Working Capital Applied To:				
Purchase warehouse			(*f*) 3,000	
Pay on long-term notes			(*g*) 6,000	
Purchase equipment			(*i*) 9,000	
Other investing activities:				
Acquired land			(*j*) 5,000	
Increase in working capital			(*k*) 10,500	
		33,500	33,500	

Entry (*d*)—Amortization of patents also is a noncash expense on the income statement. The entry made in the accounts was a debit to Patent Amortization Expense and a credit to Patents; hence, the worksheet entry is:

Working capital provided—adjustment to net income (patent amortization)	500	
Patents		500

Entry (*e*)—The entry to record the sale of equipment is a particularly important one to review. The entry in the accounts was:

Cash	3,000	
Accumulated depreciation—equipment	4,000	
Loss of sale equipment (income summary)	1,000	
Equipment		8,000

Observe that the loss of $1,000 was reported on the income statement as a *deduction;* yet the working capital *provided* amounted to $3,000 (cash received). Obviously, then, we must add the $1,000 back to net income and show the $3,000 as an item under working capital provided; the following restatement of the above entry does precisely that on the worksheet:

Working capital provided—sale of equipment	3,000	
Accumulated depreciation—equipment	4,000	
Working capital provided—adjustment to net income (loss on sale of equipment)	1,000	
Equipment		8,000

Entry (*f*)—The purchase of a warehouse for cash and a long-term note is straightforward; the entry on the worksheet is as follows:

Land	11,000	
Working capital applied—purchase of land		3,000
Long-term notes payable		8,000

Entry (*g*)—This entry as restated on the worksheet is:

Long-term notes payable	6,000	
Working capital applied—payment of long-term note		6,000

Entry (*h*)—The sale of capital stock provided working capital; the worksheet entry is:

Working capital provided—sale of capital stock	10,000	
Capital stock		10,000

Entry (*i*)—The purchase of equipment was recorded in the accounts as follows:

Equipment	9,000	
Cash		4,500
Accounts payable special (current liability)		4,500

The worksheet entry is:

Equipment	9,000	
Working capital applied (purchase of equipment)		9,000

Note that the entire amount ($9,000) represents working capital applied since the cash and liability are both working capital items; if the note had been long term, as in entry (*f*), funds applied would have been only $4,500.

Entry (*j*)—This exchange of capital stock for land was recorded in the accounts as a debit to land and a credit to capital stock for $5,000. Clearly working capital was not affected. However, it is a financing-investing activity that must be reported on the statement. Accordingly, it is incorporated on the worksheet as an "in and out" transaction. This is accomplished by making the *two* entries on the worksheet similar to what would have been done had the stock been sold for cash, which was then immediately disbursed to pay for the warehouse. The two entries on the worksheet are:

(*j*-1)	Working capital provided—capital stock issued	5,000	
	Capital stock		5,000
(*j*-2)	Land	5,000	
	Working capital applied—acquired land		5,000

Entry (*k*)—This entry is optional. It merely reflects the change in working capital and *must agree* with the change shown in Part II of the statement ($10,500 in this case).

Having taken cognizance of all of the data available prior to entry (*k*), the analyst should verify that the change on each line from the beginning trial balance to the ending trial balance has been fully accounted for. In some *problems* one or more items of data are omitted, so that the analyst must deduce the probable transaction(s) and enter them on the worksheet.

Based upon the data developed at the bottom of the worksheet, you can easily prepare the statement of sources and applications of working capital (see Illustration 21–1).

Determine whether each of the following statements is true or false.

_______ 1. The statement of changes in financial position, working capital basis, includes two parts; each part can be prepared independently of the other.

_______ 2. A company that has incurred a loss cannot have generated any working capital from operations.

_______ 3. All increases and decreases in noncurrent accounts cause changes in working capital.

_______ 4. Depreciation recorded each period is a source of working capital.

Now check your responses by comparing them with Answer Frame 2[21], page 76.

Frame 3[21]

Statement of Changes in Financial Position, Cash Basis

Management frequently faces the problem of a cash shortage, which suggests the importance of cash planning and control. Cash flow analysis parallels the analysis of working capital except that it focuses on only *one element* of working capital. Although working capital analysis as reviewed in the preceding section is useful for managerial planning and control, it fails in one major respect: it normally does not provide sufficient information relative to cash, the most *liquid* and frequently the most difficult asset to obtain. A statement of changes in financial position, working capital basis, may show a very favorable increase in working capital even though the firm has no cash at all; the current assets may be represented by noncash items such as excessive inventories and accounts receivable. For cash flow analysis it is usually desirable to define cash as being composed of cash in banks, cash on hand, and short-term investments. Short-term investments normally are included since they represent temporary employment of idle cash and can (and presumably will) be converted to cash in the near future. For these reasons a statement of changes in financial position, cash basis, is frequently preferable. A statement for AB Corporation is shown in Illustration 21–3.

The statement of changes in financial position, cash basis, shown in Illustration 21–3 presents three separate sections: (1) Sources of Cash (cash inflow), (2) Uses of Cash (cash outflow), and (3) Financing and Investing Activities Not Affecting Cash. Clearly, this statement focuses on cash flows rather than working capital flows as shown in Illustration 21–1. In common with the working capital statement it also reflects all other financing and investing activities. Thus, both statements report changes due to all financial resource inflows and outflows; as a consequence either statement is frequently referred to as an "all resources" report.

You should observe one point of difference between Illustrations 21–1 and 21–3 in respect to format.

Answer frame 2[21]

1. True. Part I of the statement of changes in financial position, working capital basis, can be prepared independently by analyses of the noncurrent accounts. Part II can be taken directly from the comparative balance sheets, that is, from a listing (e.g., a trial balance) of the beginning and ending balances of the working capital accounts.
2. False. Although the company incurred a loss, expenses such as depreciation will not have reduced working capital. Thus, when these expenses are "added back," working capital may have been generated by operations.
3. False. Changes in noncurrent accounts *may* give rise to changes in working capital accounts; every noncurrent account must be examined to see if it has changed during the period and if so, to see if its change has affected working capital.
4. False. Depreciation is not a source of working capital; it must be added back to operations, however, so that the source of working capital will be correctly reported. The reason for the "addback" results from the fact that depreciation expense reduces net income but it does not directly reduce working capital. Therefore, it does not conform to the assumption that all expenses reduce working capital.

If you missed any of the above, reread Frame 2[21] before proceeding. Then turn to Frame 3[21], page 75, and continue reading.

Frame 3[21] continued

Illustration 21–3

AB CORPORATION
Statement of Changes in Financial Position, Cash Basis
For the Month of April 19X

Sources of Cash:			
Operations:			
Reported net income (accrual basis)		$ 8,000	
Adjustments to convert income from accrual basis to cash generated (*—deductions):			
Depreciation expense	$ 5,000		
Doubtful accounts expense	1,000		
Insurance expense	2,000		
Decrease in accounts receivable	1,000		
Increase in accounts payable	1,000		
Decrease in wages payable	1,000*		
Increase in interest payable	1,000		
Increase in inventory	6,000*		
Loss on sale of fixed assets	2,000		
Net adjustment		6.000	
Cash generated by current operations		14,000	
Other sources of cash:			
Issued notes payable	20,000		
Sale of fixed assets	4,000	24,000	
Total cash provided			$38,000
Uses of Cash:			
Paid dividends		25.000	
Total cash used			25.000
Increase in cash during the month			$13,000
Add beginning balance in cash			18.000
Ending Balance in Cash			$31,000
Financing and Investing Activities Not Affecting Cash:			
Issued capital stock to acquire land			$20,000

In Illustration 21–1 the "other financing and investing activities" were reported under both captions *Sources* and *Uses* (i.e., the stock issued for land $5,000 in Illustration 21–1). In contrast, in Illustration 21–3 these types of transactions were reported under only one caption; the separate caption is entitled "Financing and Investing Activities Not Affecting Cash" (i.e., the stock issued for land $20,000 in illustration 21–3). These are two separate methods of reporting these particular items; either method could have been used in Illustrations 21–1 or 21–3. Many accountants prefer the latter method. *APB Opinion No. 19* requires that they be reported but does not prescribe the particular format.

Analytical Worksheet to Develop Statement of Changes in Financial Position, Cash Basis. Because of the relatively complex analysis that is required to develop this statement, an analytical worksheet is essential to provide an organized approach. Several worksheets have been developed for this purpose; however, the one reviewed and illustrated herein is the easiest to understand, since, as in the working capital worksheet, the relevant entries are repeated in their original format. In addition, this worksheet has the necessary flexibility to handle the most complex situations. The cash flow worksheet follows essentially the same pattern as the working capital worksheet previously reviewed. The cash flow worksheet must be designed (*a*) to convert reported net income (accrual basis) to a *cash inflow basis* (that is, cash provided by operations), (*b*) to sort out the other cash sources and cash applications, and (*c*) to identify the noncash transactions. The worksheet developed to provide data directly for the statement on a cash basis (Illustration 21–3) is shown in Illustration 21–4. The worksheet for AB Corporation was developed from the following data available from the records of the AB Corporation for the month of April 19X.

1. Income statement for the month of April 19X:

Sales		$80,000
Less: Purchases	$40,000	
Increase in inventory	6,000	34,000
		46,000
Expenses:		
Depreciation	5,000	
Doubtful accounts	1,000	
Insurance	2,000	
Interest	2,000	
Salaries and wages	12,000	
Other expenses	14,000	36,000
Net income before extraordinary items		10,000
Extraordinary items:		
Loss on sale of fixed assets		2,000
Net income		$ 8,000

2. Balance sheets (unclassified):

	March 31	*April 30*
Cash	$ 18,000	$ 31,000
Accounts receivable	30,000	28,500
Allowance for doubtful accounts	1,500*	2,000*
Inventory	10,000	16,000
Prepaid insurance	2,400	400
Fixed assets	80,000	65,000
Accumulated depreciation	20,000*	16,000*
Land	40,100	60,100
Total	$159,000	$183,000
Accounts payable	$ 10,000	$ 11,000
Wages payable	2,000	1,000
Interest payable		1,000
Long-term notes payable	20,000	40,000
Capital stock (par $10)	100,000	120,000
Retained earnings	27,000	10,000
Total	$159,000	$183,000

* Credit balance accounts.

3. Cash account:

Debits		*Credits*	
Balance	$18,000	Purchases	$10,000
Sales	20,000	Salaries and wages	5,000
Fixed assets	4,000	Accounts payable	4,000
Sales	15,000	Salaries and wages	2,000
Notes payable	20,000	Purchases	5,000
Sales	15,000	Expenses	6,000
Accounts receivable	31,000	Dividends	25,000
		Purchases	5,000
		Expenses	8,000
		Accounts payable	6,000
		Accounts payable	9,000
		Wages	6,000
		Interest	1,000

4. Retained Earnings account showed a debit for dividends, $25,000.
5. Wrote off $500 account receivable as uncollectible.

The Worksheet to Analyze Cash Sources and Applications (Illustration 21–4) was developed as follows:

Step 1—Lay out the worksheet with the following primary captions: Four amount columns:
1. Beginning balances.
2. Analysis of interim entries, debit.
3. Analysis of interim entries, credit.
4. Ending balances.

Five side captions:
1. Cash.
2. Noncash accounts (from balance sheet).
3. Cash provided by (subdivided between "operations" and "other sources").
4. Cash applied to.
5. Noncash investing and financing activities.

Step 2—Enter the beginning and ending balance sheet amounts in the first and last columns.

Step 3—Enter on the worksheet under the two columns for Analysis of Interim Entries certain summary entries made in the accounts during the period so as to account for the change on each line from the beginning to ending balances. The entries to be recorded on the worksheet are (*a*) to close net income to retained earnings, (*b*) to convert net income to cash flow basis, and (*c*) to account for all other entries affecting the balance sheet accounts. The relevant entries are indicated on the worksheet (Illustration 21–4); each entry is explained below.

The worksheet is designed so that *all data* needed for the *statement* are "pulled out" at the bottom of the worksheet. The entries on the worksheet must be *selected* from the income statement and the worksheet data.

Entry (*a*)—The original entry made in the accounts for net income (closing) was a debit to Income Summary and a credit to Retained Earnings. Since net income generates cash, the worksheet entry is:

Cash provided—operations (net income)	8,000	
Retained earnings		8,000

Entry (*b*)—The original entry for depreciation made in the accounts debited Depreciation Expense and credited Accumulated Depreciation. Since depreciation expense is a *noncash* deduction on the income statement, it must be "added back" to net income to convert that figure to a *cash flow basis.* Accordingly, the entry is adapted on the worksheet as follows:

Cash provided—operations (depreciation)	5,000	
Accumulated depreciation		5,000

Illustration 21–4

AB CORPORATION
Worksheet to Develop the Statement of Changes in Financial Position, Cash Basis
For the Month of April 19X

	Balances March 31	Analysis of Interim Entries		Balances April 30
		Debit	Credit	
Debits				
Cash	18,000	(*n*) 13,000		31,000
Noncash Accounts:				
Accounts receivable	30,000		(*e*) 1,500	28,500
Inventory	10,000	(*i*) 6,000		16,000
Prepaid insurance	2,400		(*d*) 2,000	400
Fixed assets	80,000		(*j*) 15,000	65,000
Land	40,100	(*l*) 20,000		60,100
	180.500			201,000
Credits				
Allowance for doubtful accounts	1,500	(*e*) 500	(*c*) 1,000	2,000
Accumulated depreciation	20,000	(*j*) 9,000	(*b*) 5,000	16,000
Accounts payable	10,000		(*f*) 1,000	11,000
Wages payable	2,000	(*g*) 1,000		1,000
Interest payable			(*h*) 1,000	1,000
Long-term notes payable	20,000		(*k*) 20,000	40,000
Capital stock (par $10)	100,000		(*l*) 20,000	120,000
Retained earnings	27.000	(*m*) 25.000	(*a*) 8.000	10,000
	180.500	74,500	74.500	201,000
Cash Provided By:				
Operations:				
Net income		(*a*) 8,000		
Adjustments:				
Depreciation expense		(*b*) 5,000		
Doubtful accounts expense		(*c*) 1,000		
Insurance expense		(*d*) 2,000		
Decrease in accounts receivable		(*e*) 1,000		
Increase in accounts payable		(*f*) 1,000		
Decrease in wages payable			(*g*) 1,000	
Increase in interest payable		(*h*) 1,000		
Increase in inventory			(*i*) 6,000	
Loss on sale of fixed assets		(*j*) 2,000		
Other sources of cash:				
Sale of fixed assets		(*j*) 4,000		
Issued notes payable—long term		(*k*) 20,000		
Cash Applied To:				
Dividends			(*m*) 25,000	
Increase in cash during period			(*n*) 13,000	
Noncash Investing and Financing Activities:				
Issued stock to acquire land		(*l*) 20,000	(*l*) 20.000	
		65,000	65.000	

Entry (*c*)—The amount of bad debt expense on the income statement is another *noncash* expense; therefore, the worksheet entry would be:

Cash provided—operations (doubtful accounts expense)	1,000	
Allowance for doubtful accounts		1,000

Entry (*d*)—Since the insurance premium when paid was debited to Prepaid Insurance, an adjustment was made in the accounts for expired insurance. This adjustment involved a debit to Insurance Expense and a credit to Prepaid Insurance; thus insurance expense is also a *noncash* expense on the income statement (the payment of premium was shown as a cash application in the period paid rather than in the period used). Therefore, the worksheet entry must be:

Cash provided—operations (insurance expense)	2,000	
Prepaid insurance		2,000

Entry (*e*)—Inspection of the worksheet indicates that accounts receivable decreased $1,500 during the year; however, $500 of that decrease was due to the write off of a bad account. The additional $1,000 decrease in accounts receivable therefore must result from cash collection of accounts receivable in addition to the cash collections on sales that are included in net income; consequently, the worksheet entry must be:

Allowance for doubtful accounts	500	
Cash provided—operations (decrease in accounts receivable)	1,000	
Accounts receivable		1,500

Entry (*f*)—Inspection of the worksheet indicates that accounts payable increased $1,000 during the period. Since this change affects the cash flow from operations, the worksheet entry would be:

Cash provided—operations (increase in accounts payable)	1,000	
Accounts payable		1,000

Entry (*g*)—Inspection of the worksheet indicates a decrease in wages payable; since this reflects a cash outlay for wages in addition to the cash outlays implicitly included in wages expense on the income statement, the original entry must be restated as follows:

Wages payable	1,000	
Cash provided—operations (decrease in wages payable)		1,000

Note—Particular attention is called to this entry since it results in a *credit* under cash provided. It will be recalled that cash provided items normally are debits; what we have here is a negative cash provided item. That is, it is a *subtraction* from net income to convert to a cash inflow basis.

Entry (*h*)—Inspection of the worksheet indicates an increase in interest payable; this is the same type of entry as (*g*) except that it goes the other way (an increase). Therefore, the worksheet entry is:

Cash provided—operations (increase in interest payable)	1,000	
Interest payable		1,000

Entry (*i*)—There was a $6,000 increase in inventory, which affects cash inflow from net income; therefore, the worksheet entry is:

Inventory	6,000	
Cash provided—operations (inventory increase)		6,000

Entry (*j*)—Fixed assets costing $15,000 were sold (accumulated depreciation $9,000) for cash of $4,000. The resultant loss of $2,000 was deducted from net income, which must be "corrected" to a cash basis; the sale provided a cash inflow of $4,000. The entry to record the sale is restated on the working papers as follows:

Cash provided—other sources (sale of fixed assets)	4,000	
Cash provided—operations (adjustment for loss on sale of fixed assets)	2,000	
Accumulated depreciation	9,000	
Fixed assets		15,000

Entry (*k*)—Borrowing on long-term liabilities represents a source of cash.

Cash provided—other sources (issued long-term liability)	20,000	
Long-term notes payable		20,000

Entry (*l*)—The purchase of land by the issuance of capital stock did not represent an application of cash. Rather this is a noncash financing and investing activity which must be reported on the statement. Therefore, two companion entries are made on the worksheet (as was done in Illustration 21–2):

Noncash financing activity	20,000	
Capital stock		20,000
Land	20,000	
Noncash investing activity		20,000

Entry (*m*)—The payment of cash dividends represents a cash application.

Retained earnings	5,000	
Cash applied—cash dividend		5,000

Entry (*n*)—Now that all differences between the beginning and ending balances entered on the worksheet have been accounted for, a final (although optional) entry may be made to "clear the cash line" and to "balance" the lower section of the worksheet; this entry tends to check the accuracy of the work.

Cash (to balance)	13,000	
Cash applied (increase during the period)		13,000

The statement of changes in financial position, cash basis (Illustration 21–3), now can be taken directly from the bottom portion of the worksheet. Note that both statements and the worksheet arrive at the same $13,000 increase in cash during the period; this point serves as a check on the accuracy of the analyses.

True or false?

______ 1. Where the statement of changes in financial position reports a substantial increase in working capital, it clearly indicates that the company does not have a cash shortage.

______ 2. In Illustration 21–3, the addback for "Increase in accounts payable" reflects the addback for some expense such as purchases which did not reduce cash.

______ 3. In Illustration 21–3, the deduction for "Decreases in wages payable" reflects a deduction for wage expense that has not yet been paid.

______ 4. If a firm incurred $5,000 of income tax expense of which $3,000 was paid in cash, $1,000 was currently payable and $1,000 was deferred due to income tax allocation procedures, it would be necessary to add back to net income $2,000 in arriving at cash provided by operations.

Now check your responses by comparing them with Answer Frame 3[21], page 82.

Answer frame 3[21]

1. False. The increase in working capital may be due to increases in noncash items. For example, the current assets may be represented by mostly noncash items such as inventories, receivables, and prepaid items, and there may be a cash deficit. Furthermore, cash could have been used to pay current liabilities.
2. True. In this sense, the addback for "Increase in accounts payable" is identical to the depreciation expense addback.
3. False. The deduction for "Decreases in wages payable" represents a cash payment of the liability. Recall that it is assumed that Wages Expense for the period reduced cash. Therefore, if Wages Payable was also reduced during the period, the summary journal entry to reflect all wages for the period would be (assuming wages expense on the income statement was $12,000):

Wages expense	12,000	
Wages payable	1,000	
Cash		13,000

   Thus, this added deduction of $1,000 is needed to reflect the total cash effect on operations of all transactions involving wages.
4. True. The cash reduction for income taxes was only $3,000. However, net income was reduced by the full $5,000. Therefore, $2,000 would be added back to net income in arriving at cash provided by operations.

If you missed any of the above questions, reread Frame 3[21] before proceeding. You have now completed Chapter 21. Now turn to page 123 and work Examination 5. Then continue reading with Chapter 22.

chapter 22

PENSIONS AND LEASES

Frame 1[22]

Accounting Problems Created by Pension Plans

A pension plan is an arrangement whereby an employer provides for financial benefits for retired employees. The costs of pension plans are expenses to the employer. Thus, there are three primary accounting problems posed by pension plans: (1) determination of the *amount* of the cost, (2) selection of the appropriate *periods* (timing) in which to record the amount as an expense, and (3) reporting of information in respect to the pension plan on the periodic financial statements.

Determination of Cost of Pension Plans

Basically, pension plans are paid for by the employer under one of two arrangements. One type of arrangement is that by which the employer pays the financial benefits directly to the retired employee. In this case the actual amount of cash disbursed is the cost; but there is still the critical problem as to the timing of the *deduction* as an expense on the income statement, since pension payments in this situation usually are for *past services* rendered by the employee. Under the other type of arrangement, the employer enters into a contract with an outside trustee (usually an insurance company) whereby the employer pays a periodic *premium* and, in return, the insurance company assumes the liability for all pension payments to the retired employees. In this case, the premium payments constitute the cost; however, the central question remains as to when the cost should be reported on the income statement.

Determination of Timing of Pension Costs

The usual situation for a pension plan is to establish it on a funded basis with an outside party; that is, the employer makes periodic payments to a trustee in sufficient amounts to meet the future demands for funds to disburse to the employees after retirement. Thus a pension plan causes the incurrence of a periodic expense that is related to the pension benefits being earned by each employee. Two types of pension plan costs must be recorded in the accounts and reported on the financial statements, viz:

1. Normal pension cost. The amount of cost, on an accrual basis, that should be assigned each period to the pension plan for *current* services of the employees. The amount of this cost is computed by an actuary since it is based upon many factors such as age of employee, retirement age, income, expected life (from mortality tables), employee turnover rates, and expected interest rates. This cost will be recorded each year as long as the pension plan is in effect. To illustrate, assume that the actuary computed the normal pension cost for the year 19A to be $40,000. The following accounting entry would be made:

Pension expense—normal service cost	40,000	
Cash (payment to trustee)		40,000

Interest earned on the fund from date of deposit to date of payment as benefits to the retired employee serve to increase the amount in the pension fund; this interest does not accrue directly to the employer; however, it does serve to reduce Pension Expense because of the interest factor.

2. Past service cost. A company would incur this type of pension cost only if it started a pension plan after the company was first organized. Of course, most pension plans are initiated some years subsequent to the organization date. This is a "catch-up" amount that must be paid into the pension fund soon after its inception in order to provide pension credits for employees of the company for their years of service prior to the inception of the pension plan. It is a one-time cost that is computed by the actuary at date of inception of the plan. To illustrate, assume at the date of inception of the above pension plan on January 1, 19A, that the actuary determined the past service cost to be $70,000. This amount of cash must be paid into the fund immediately, or alternatively on an installment basis including an agreed-upon interest charge. Assuming that the employer decided to make a single payment, the past service cost on January 1, 19A, would be recorded as follows:

Deferred pension expense—past service cost	70,000	
Cash		70,000

At the end of each year for the next ten years an adjusting entry could be made as follows:

Pension expense—past service cost	7,000	
Deferred pension expense—past service cost		7,000

The effect of this procedure would be to amortize or spread the past service cost over the next ten years on a straight-line basis. In accordance with *APB Opinion No. 8* most companies amortize the past service cost over ten years on an interest (i.e., present value) basis. Also most companies elect to pay the cash required (i.e., the $70,000) on an installment basis, say over ten years. The above illustrative pension plan can be diagrammed to facilitate understanding as follows:

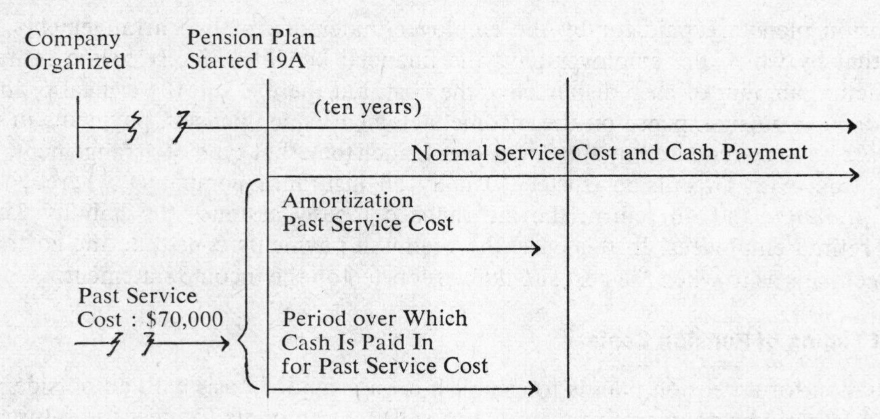

Assuming that the employer decided to pay in the $70,000 past service cost over a ten-year period, and assuming a 6% interest rate the installment payment each year would be:

Annual payment = $70,000 ÷ present value of annuity of 1 for 10 rents at 6% (Table 6–4)
= $70,000 ÷ 7.3600871
= $9,510.75 (per year)

Therefore, the annual entry for pension costs (assuming normal cost of $40,000) would be:

Pension expense—normal service cost	40,000.00	
Pension expense—past service cost	9,510.75	
Cash		49,510.75

This procedure amortizes the past service pension cost over ten years on the interest or present value basis and records the cost of the pension plan, including the interest charge, as a cash disbursement. The past service cost as recorded each year will be constant; in contrast the normal pension cost each year will vary depending upon the computations of the actuary. Some accountants feel that the past service cost should be debited to retained earnings rather than to period expense for a period of time in the future (i.e., ten years in the above example). This position is supported by the argument that Past Service Cost, by definition, pertains to prior periods the incomes of which were not charged for the pension expense that the employer did in fact incur. Other accountants favor recognition of past service cost over the current and future periods on the theory that current implementation of the plan is a current decision with current and future effects on the resources of the employer. *APB Opinion No. 8* adopted the latter position. The *Opinion* also requires disclosure of all important aspects of the pension plan by way of footnotes to the financial statements. In addition, the *Opinion* identified minimum and maximum limits on annual pension expense to be recognized by the employer.

The defined minimum from *APB Opinion No. 8* is the total of:

1. Normal service cost.
2. Accrued interest expense on *unfunded* past service cost.
3. Provision for vested benefits, those pension benefits an employee can keep if he or she leaves the employment of the company prior to reaching retirement age.

The defined maximum is the total of:

1. Normal service cost.
2. Ten percent of the past service cost.
3. Ten percent of any additional cost arising from amendments to the pension plan.
4. Accrued interest expense on any unfunded pension expense.

In 1974 the U.S. Congress passed the Pension Reform Act. With a few exceptions which are beyond the scope of this book, the Reform Act did not affect the accounting for pension expense. The major thrust of the Reform Act was to require more stringent funding practices by employer companies because a large number of companies were operating on a "pay-as-you-go" basis and not funding pension expenses as they occurred. The new requirements were instituted primarily to protect employees rather than to correct accounting abuses.

Indicate whether each of the following statements is true or false by writing *T* or *F* in the space provided.

______ 1. In general, pension plans may be on a funded or unfunded basis.

______ 2. Normal pension cost and past service cost will be recorded each year that a pension plan is in effect.

______ 3. Companies generally amortize past service pension cost on a straight-line basis.

______ 4. Retained earnings should not be debited directly for past service pension cost.

Now check your answers by comparing them with Answer Frame 1[22], page 86.

Frame 2[22]

Accounting for Leases

A lease is a conveyance of specific property by a lessor to a lessee in return for an agreed rent or other compensation. The period of time may be short or long, and the rent may be paid under a variety of arrangements as agreed upon by the two parties. A lease results in an expense to the *lessee* (tenant) and

Answer frame 1[22]

1. False. Since passage of the Pension Reform Act of 1974, pension plans must, in general, be funded by payments to an independent trustee.
2. False. Although normal pension cost would be recorded each year the plan is in effect, past service cost often would not be. A pension plan established at the time a company begins operations would not record past service costs. Also, companies which incur past service cost must amortize the cost over a number of years. After the amortization period, only normal pension costs would be recorded.
3. False. *APB Opinion No. 8* requires amortization of the past service cost on an interest or present value basis.
4. True. *APB Opinion No. 8* specifies that past service pension cost will be allocated to future periods, specifically between 10 and 40 years. Furthermore, it is not to be shown as an extraordinary item in the income statement.

If you missed any of the above, you should restudy Frame 1[22] before turning to Frame 2[22], page 85.

Frame 2[22] continued

a revenue to the *lessor* (owner). The right of the lessee to use the property under the lease agreement usually is referred to as a leasehold. Improvements (capital additions) added to leased property by the lessee usually are designated as *leasehold improvements.* Accounting for leases depends in large part upon the specifications of the lease contract. Most leases come under one of the two basic categories: operating leases and financing leases.

Operating Leases

These are typically short-term, year-to-year leases involving a monthly or annual rental, such as the case where a certified public accountant leases a suite of offices in a large office building at $1,000 per month. However, they may also be long-term noncancelable leases which fail to meet the criteria for classifying the lease as a financing lease. Those criteria are covered in the next section. Both the lessor and lessee account for the rent and related items on an accrual basis, as reviewed in prior chapters. There are no unique or complex accounting problems involved. To illustrate, the entry each month for this operating lease would be:

Rent expense	1,000	
Cash		1,000

Occasionally a longer term lease may call for a lump-sum prepayment of part or all of the lease cost, as in the case of rental of a building on January 1, 19A, for three years for $6,000 down plus annual rentals of $10,000 payable on each January 1. Lump-sum rental payments no longer are common, in view of the income tax laws which require that the entire lump sum be reported as income in the year collected by the lessor. In most leases of this type the only unique accounting problem relates to the treatment of the prepayment; theoretically it should be allocated over the life of the lease. Two approaches to amortization of the prepayment are utilized, the straight-line and the present value methods.

a. Straight-line amortization is the simpler approach, but it is not theoretically preferable. To illustrate, the entries by the lessee for the first year of the lease contract outlined above would be:

January 1, 19A—To record payment of the lump sum:

Prepaid rent expense	6,000	
Cash		6,000

January 1, 19A—To record first annual rental:

Rent expense	10,000	
Cash		10,000

December 31, 19A—To record straight-line amortization of prepaid rent expense for first period:

Rent expense	2,000	
Prepaid rent expense ($6,000 ÷ 3 years)		2,000

b. Present value amortization is the theoretically preferable procedure. It utilizes compound interest concepts, as reviewed and illustrated in Chapter 6; the entries would be essentially the same as above except for the *amounts*. To illustrate present value amortization, assuming a 6% interest rate and amortization at year-end (i.e., an ordinary annuity), the periodic amortization to rent expense for the $6,000 prepayment would be as follows[1]:

Rent expense = $6,000 ÷ Present value of annuity of 1 for 3 rents at 6% (Table 6–4)
= $6,000 ÷ 2.6730120
= $2,244.66

We can now prepare a table of amortization that indicates the entries, viz:

Period	Periodic Rent	Interest (6%)	Amortization of Prepayment	Unamortized Balance
1-1-19A				$6,000.00
12-31-19A	$2,244.66	$360.00	$1,884.66	4,115.34
12-31-19B	2,244.66	246.92	1,997.74	2,117.60
12-31-19C	2,244.66	127.06	2,117.60	–0–

Based upon the above table the entries for the first year would be:

January 1, 19A—To record prepayment of the lump sum:

Prepaid rent expense	6,000	
Cash		6,000

January 1, 19A—To record first annual rental:

Rent expense	10,000	
Cash		10,000

December 31, 19A—To record amortization of prepaid rent expense for first period:

Rent expense	2,244.66	
Interest revenue		360.00
Prepaid rent expense		1,884.66

Financing Leases

A long-term lease arrangement that passes from the lessor to the lessee most of the risks and rewards of ownership of the leased property is referred to as a financing lease.[2] The dominant characteristics of *financing* leases are those of a financing transaction as in a sale of property even though the

---

[1] Even though rent is customarily paid in advance, it is a prepayment at the moment it is paid. The rent in this example becomes expense over the three years covered by the rental agreement. For this reason, this prepayment is construed to be an ordinary annuity, which assumes that the expense occurs at the end of each period covered by the rental agreement. The contrary position, that the rent becomes expense at the beginning of each year, can also be defended. That situation creates an annuity due.

[2] The authoritative document on accounting for leases, FASB *Statement No. 13,* uses the category *direct financing leases* to refer to a more narrowly defined type of lease, which is explained below. Here, however, the general category *financing* leases is used for convenience to refer to all leases other than *operating* leases.

lessor retains title to the property. For example, assume that lessor and lessee execute a financing lease. The lessee will be compelled to capitalize the leased property and record a lease liability as though the property were being purchased outright. And the lessor will reciprocate by removing the leased asset from his or her accounts and by replacing it with a Gross Investment in Leases (i.e., a lease receivable) account. It should be clear that the amount at which the lease transaction is recorded by both parties is the present value of the future lease payments.

The material that follows incorporates the provisions of FASB *Statement No. 13,* "Accounting for Leases," issued November 1976. The issues in lease accounting center upon the distinction between operating and financing leases. FASB *Statement No. 13* delineates leases by type more specifically, however, as indicated below.

	Specific Type of Lease, from Perspective of:	
General Type of Lease	*Lessee*	*Lessor*
Operating	Operating	Operating
Financing	Capital	Direct financing or sales type

Criteria for Identifying Leases

In order to qualify as a capital lease from the lessee's perspective, and a sales-type or direct financing lease from the lessor's perspective, the lease must be *noncancelable.* The additional criteria for the *lessee* that distinguish a *capital* lease from an *operating* lease may be stated as follows: If the lease agreement meets any *one* of the following four provisions, the lessee has a capital lease. Otherwise, the lease is operating.

1. Lease transfers title to leased property to the lessee by end of lease term.
2. Lease contains a bargain purchase option.
3. Lease term covers 75% or more of the estimated economic life of leased property.
4. The present value, at the beginning of the lease term, of the minimum lease payment equals or exceeds 90% of the excess of the fair value of the leased property to the lessor at the inception of the lease over any related investment tax credit retained by the lessor.

Criteria 3 and 4 are not used if the lease begins during the last 25% of the *total* estimated economic life of the leased property.

The criteria for identifying *sales-type* and *direct financing* leases from the *lessor's* perspective include:

a. Meet any one of the above criteria for the lessee's capital lease, plus both of the following:
b. Lessor is reasonably assured of collecting lease payments from the lessee, and
c. No material cost uncertainties exist as to the lessor's unreimbursable future outlays under the lease agreement.

Thus, if the *lease fails to meet either one* of these criteria, the lessor will treat the lease as *operating.*

If the lease agreement does meet the above criteria, the lessor must then determine whether the lease is a *sales-type* or a *direct financing* lease. The criteria for making this distinction are:

(1) If the fair value of the leased property at the inception of the lease is greater than or less than its carrying amount (typically cost), a profit or loss is recognized, and the lease is sales type to the lessor.

(2) If the fair value and the carrying amount of the leased property are the same, the lease is direct financing to the lessor.

FASB *Statement No. 13* gives technical meanings to several key terms.

1. *Fair value* of leased property is the price for which the property could be sold in an arm's-length transaction between unrelated parties. When the lessor is a manufacturer or dealer that markets its products via leases, the fair value will ordinarily be its normal selling price. When the lessor is not a manufacturer or dealer, the fair value will ordinarily be the cost of the property, unless a significant amount of time has lapsed between the lessor's acquisition of the property and the inception of the lease. In this case, fair value must be determined in light of current market conditions at the inception of the lease.
2. *Estimated residual value* of leased property is the estimated fair value at the end of the lease term.
3. *Minimum lease payments* include (*a*) minimum rental payments and (*b*) guarantee by the lessee of the residual value of the leased property.
4. *Interest rate implicit in the lease* is the discount rate used to reduce gross minimum lease payments to their present values. This *implicit rate* is the rate which, when applied to the minimum lease payments, causes the aggregate present value thereof at the beginning of the lease term to be equal to the fair value of the leased property at the inception of the lease. The *lessor* will use this *implicit rate* as the discount rate in present value computations.
5. *Lessee's incremental borrowing rate* is the rate that at the inception of the lease, the lessee would have incurred to borrow funds necessary to have purchased the leased property. The *lessee* will use this rate only for purposes of determining whether the lease meets the lessee's Criterion 4.

A final stipulation is that the lessee will not capitalize leased property at a present value (of future lease payments) in excess of the fair value of the property at the inception of the lease.

True or false?

_______ 1. Periodic payments on short-term leases should be expensed as they are made.

_______ 2. Noncancelable leases should never be accounted for as operating leases.

_______ 3. A lease agreement which transfers title (to the leased property) to the lessee before the end of the lease term is automatically a capital lease to the lessee and either a sales-type or a direct-financing lease to the lessor.

_______ 4. If the fair value of leased property (at the date a lease agreement is executed) exceeds the lessor's carrying value for the property, an element of gross margin (profit) is indicated and hence it is a sales-type lease to the lessor.

_______ 5. If the lessee has a capital lease, then the lessor automatically has either a sales-type or a direct-financing lease.

Now compare your responses with Answer Frame 2[22], page 90.

Frame 3[22]

The above guidelines will now be incorporated into a set of illustrative entries for both the lessor and the lessee. Assume that LR, Inc., the lessor, paid $5,000 for an automobile that has a fair value of $5,500 and an estimated economic life of five years. LR, Inc. leases the automobile to LE, Inc., for a fixed noncancelable term of 2½ years beginning on January 1, 19A, with rentals of $1,232 due at the beginning of each six-month period. Residual value of the automobile at the end of the lease is expected to be zero, and LE, Inc., makes no related guarantee. LE, Inc., pays the normal expenses of maintenance and taxes. No investment tax credit is available. LE, Inc., depreciates its own automobiles on a straight-line basis.

Answer frame 2[22]

1. True. Payments on short-term leases should be expensed as they are made. Deferrals or accruals will be necessary if the payment date is different from the end of the fiscal period.
2. False. If a noncancelable lease fails to meet certain criteria, it is classified as an *operating* lease—even though it is noncancelable.
3. False. This lease is automatically a capital lease to the lessee, but the lease agreement must meet two additional criteria (*b* and *c* on page 88) before the lessor classifies the lease as other than an operating lease.
4. True. This difference between fair (sales) value and carrying (book) value indicates gross margin (profit) to the lessor. Conditional on having met the earlier criteria given for classifying lessor's lease as other than operating, this gross margin (profit) qualifies the lease as sales-type for the lessor.
5. False. Note that the lessor's criteria for classifying a lease as other than operating (i.e., as sales-type or direct-financing) include two additional provisions (*b* and *c* on page 88) in addition to those used by the lessee to classify a lease as capital.

If you missed any of the above questions, you should reread Frame 2[22] before proceeding. Then continue reading Frame 3[22], page 89.

Frame 3[22] continued

LE, Inc., has an incremental borrowing rate of 10% per year. LR, Inc., expects to receive all the lease payments from LE, Inc., and has no material cost uncertainties.

Step 1. Now we may proceed to identify the lease type involved in the problem. The first three criteria are relatively straightforward, but Criterion 4 requires some present value computations using the minimum lease payments. In this case, the minimum lease payments are comprised solely of rentals in the amount of \$6,160 (5 × \$1,232).

LE, Inc., discounts the minimum lease payments to their present value using the incremental borrowing rate of 5% per six-month period, and compares the result to 90% of the fair value of the leased property. The present value computations are given below:[3]

$$\text{Rentals } \$1{,}232 \times 4.5460 \left(P_{\substack{n=5 \\ i=5\%}} \times 1.05 \right) = \$5{,}601$$

Even though the present value of the lease payments is \$5,601, LE, Inc., will capitalize the leased asset at a maximum equal to its fair value (\$5,500)—*if the lease qualifies as a capital lease.*

From the lessee's perspective, the lease agreement fails to qualify on the first three criteria. But it does qualify on Criterion 4 inasmuch as the present value of the minimum lease payments (\$5,601) exceeds 90% of the fair value (\$5,500) of the leased property. Therefore, the *lessee* has a *capital lease.*

From the lessor's perspective, the lease will be a sales-type lease because:

1. The present value of minimum future lease payments exceeds 90% of the fair value of the leased property. (This is the same Criterion 4 used above for the lessee.) For the *lessor,* however, the *appropriate discount rate* is the *rate implicit in the lease.* In this hypothetical example, this rate turns out to be 12% per year (6% per six months). In most cases, this rate will be set by the lessor based on market conditions and then used to determine the periodic rental payments. This is shown below:[4]

[3] Refer to footnote 2. That situation involved a prepayment that was amortized over three years, thereby creating an annuity problem. The situation covered in this footnote also involves annuities in that semiannual rentals are actually paid here. Because they are paid at the beginning of each period and are assumed to become expense immediately, this situation is construed to be an annuity due. As pointed out in footnote 2, however, the rental situation can be construed to be either an ordinary annuity or an annuity due, depending on the assumed timing of the expense recognition.

[4] The astute reader will observe from (*a*) the definition of the rate implicit in the lease and (*b*) the FASB requirement that the lessors use this implicit rate as the discount rate in the present value computations, that lessors' leases will normally meet Criterion 4 above.

Fair value of leased property	$5,500
Present value of 5 semiannual rents due of 1 each at 6%	÷4.465*
Semiannual rent payments	$1,232

* $P_{n=5,\, i=6\%} \times 1.06$ (see Table 6–4).

2. LR, Inc., expects to receive all rentals from LE, Inc., and has no material cost uncertainties.
3. Fair value of leased property ($5,500) exceeds cost ($5,000).

Step 2. At this point we can prepare an amortization table which will facilitate making the journal entries for both parties to the lease. The implicit rate of 6% per six months is used for both lessor and lessee.

Date	*Periodic Lease Amount*	*Interest*	*Principal Reduction*	*Unamortized Balance*
1/1/19A				$5,500
1/1/19A	$1,232		$1,232	4,268[a]
7/1/19A	1,232	$256[b]	976[c]	3,292[d]
1/1/19B	1,232	198	1,034	2,258
7/1/19B	1,232	135	1,097	1,161
1/1/19C	1,232	71	1,161	–0–
	$6,160	$660	$5,500	

[a] $5,500 − $1,232 = $4,268
[b] $4,268 × .06 = $256
[c] $1,232 − $256 = $976
[d] $4,268 − $976 = $3,292

Step 3. The final step is to make the entries. They are given in parallel columns.

a. To record execution of the lease agreement on January 1, 19A:

LR, Inc.	Dr.	Cr.	LE, Inc.	Dr.	Cr.
Cash (first rental)	1,232		Leased property (fair value)	5,500	
Gross investment in sales-type lease (4 × $1,232) . . .	4,928		Deferred lease expense ($6,160 − $5,500)	660	
Sales (fair value)		5,500	Cash (first rental)		1,232
Unearned lease revenue ($6,160 − $5,500) . . .		660	Lease liability (4 × $1,232) . . .		4,928

b. To remove LR, Inc.'s cost of property leased (sold) from the automobile account on January 1, 19A (assuming automobile has no accumulated depreciation):

LR, Inc.	Dr.	Cr.	LE, Inc.
Cost of goods sold	5,000		(no entry)
Automobiles		5,000	

c. To record accrual of interest and second rental, on July 1, 19A:

LR, Inc.	Dr.	Cr.	LE, Inc.	Dr.	Cr.
Unearned lease revenue	256		Lease expense	256	
Lease revenue		256	Deferred lease expense		256
Cash	1,232		Lease liability	1,232	
Gross investment in sales-type lease		1,232	Cash		1,232

d. To record depreciation on the automobile at December 31, 19A (2½-year lease term, straight line, no residual value):

LR, Inc.	LE, Inc.	Dr.	Cr.
(no entry)	Depreciation expense ($5,500 ÷ 2½)	2,200	
	Leased property		2,200

The entries for 19B and 19C are similar to the entries (*c*)and (*d*) given above and, except for the depreciation entry, may also be taken directly from the amortization table above.

If the *automobile* in the above example had *cost LR, Inc., $5,500,* and if all other facts were held constant, LR, Inc. (the lessor), would have had a *direct financing* lease. In that case LE, Inc.'s entries would not have been affected by the change. However, LR, Inc.'s entries (*a*) and (*b*) would be modified as follows:

a. To record execution of lease agreement on January 1, 19A:

Cash	1,232		(no change for lessee)
Gross investment in direct financing lease	4,928		
Automobile		5,500	
Unearned lease revenue		660	

b. No entry would be needed on LR, Inc.'s books for the cost of goods sold because the cost of the automobile was removed from the Automobile account in the entry to record execution of the lease agreement. Moreover, there was no profit to recognize at the initial date.

Entries (*c*) and (*d*) would be the same as those given above for both lessor and lessee.

Assuming the sales-type lease for LR, Inc., the two companies will report the following on their financial statements at December 31, 19A, pertaining to the lease agreement:

LR, Inc.

Balance Sheet:	
Current Assets:	
Gross investment in sales-type lease	$2,464
Less: Unearned revenue	333
Net investment in lease	2,131
Noncurrent Assets:	
Gross investment in sales-type lease	1,232
Less: Unearned revenue	71
Net investment in lease	1,161
Income Statement:	
Sales	5,500
Cost of sales	5,000
Gross profit	500
Other Revenue:	
Lease revenue ($256 + $198)	454

LE, Inc.

Balance Sheet:		
Leased property under capital leases less Accumulated amortization of $2,200		
Automobiles		$3,300
Current Liabilities:		
Lease liability	2,464	
Less: Deferred lease expense	333	
	2,131	
Long-Term Liabilities:		
Lease liability	1,232	
Less: Deferred lease expense	71	
	1,161	
Income Statement:		
Operating Expenses:		
Depreciation	2,200	
Lease ($256 + $198)	454	

In addition to the above disclosure in the columnar portion of the financial statements, lessors and lessees are also required by FASB *Statement No. 13* to make certain footnote disclosures. The most significant of these are given below.

Lessors with *sales-type or direct financing* leases should report (*a*) future minimum lease receivables for each of the five succeeding fiscal years and (*b*) total contingent rentals (i.e., dependent on factors other than the passage of time) included in income for each period for which an income statement is presented. *Lessors* with *operating* leases should report the cost and carrying value, if different, of property on lease in addition to items (*a*) and (*b*) listed above for lessors with sales-type or direct financing leases.

Lessees with *capital leases* should report (*a*) the total of minimum sublease rentals to be received under noncancelable subleases and (*b*) total contingent rentals actually incurred. *Lessees* with *operating leases* should report (*a*) future minimum rental payables for each of the five succeeding years, (*b*) total minimum sublease rentals to be received under noncancelable subleases, (*c*) rental expense if not shown in the columnar portion of the income statement, and (*d*) a general description of the lessee's leasing arrangements.

Sale and Leaseback

A fairly common leasing arrangement is the sale and leaseback, in which a company (LE Company) acquires some property, including land, and sells the property to another company (LR Company). Then LR Company leases the property to LE Company. The advantage of such an arrangement is that it enables the seller/lessee, LE Company, to deduct from its taxable income the full lease payments it makes, including the portion allocable to the land. If LE Company had merely retained the property without selling it and leasing it back, it would have been able to deduct from its taxable income only the depreciation expense on the building.

Leveraged Leases

Another recent development in leasing is the leveraged lease. The leverage refers to the fact that lessors can frequently borrow from 50% to 80% of the purchase price of a leased asset and thereby reduce their own investment to the complementary 50% to 20%, respectively. Therefore, leveraged leases typically involve three parties, including a lending institution. The terms of leveraged leases are subject to negotiation and therefore vary widely.

In one fairly common type of leveraged lease, the lending institution loans funds to the lessor pursuant to the lessor's acquiring rental property. Such loans are frequently structured in such a way as to provide the lender with the *investment tax credit* plus the tax benefit of accelerated depreciation on the leased property. In exchange for these tax benefits, the lender gives the lessor/borrower a favorable interest rate on the loan.

In another fairly common type of leveraged lease, the lessor retains the leased asset for tax purposes and depreciates the asset using an accelerated depreciation method. The lessor can also deduct as a credit from the income tax liability in the year the asset is placed in service up to 10% of the cost of the asset. This is referred to as the *investment tax credit.* It is this pattern of early tax write-offs that produces a net cash inflow pattern for the lessor. Of course, the investment tax credit is a one-time credit, and in the later years of the use of the leased asset, there is little accelerated depreciation to use to reduce taxes in those years. Nevertheless, the present value considerations make the leveraged lease attractive from the lessor's viewpoint.

Determine whether each of the following statements is true or false.

______ 1. Interest expense recognized on a capital lease, when amortized, decreases in amount each period over the term of the lease.

______ 2. Both lessor and lessee may use the same amortization table for purposes of recording lease transactions.

______ 3. If the lessee has a capital lease, the lessee will record an asset. Subsequently, the lessee will depreciate the asset as though the asset were purchased.

______ 4. Lease receivable (of the lessor) should be separated into current and long-term portions in the same manner that other current assets and liabilities should be separated.

______ 5. The sale and leaseback arrangement offers distinct advantages to the lessor.

Now check your responses by referring to Answer Frame 3[22], page 94.

Answer frame 3[22]

1. True. The amount of interest expense (related to a capital lease) decreases each period because the principal balance on which the interest is based is decreasing.
2. True. Lessor's lease receipt, interest revenue, and recovery of cost are direct counterparts to lessee's lease payment, interest expense, and payment of lease liability, respectively.
3. True. A lessee's accounting for their participation in a capital lease is essentially the same as the accounting for assets formally acquired via purchase. This is the intended purpose specified in FASB Statement No. 13, i.e., to bring the lessee's accounting for capital leases in conformity with the economic reality of such leases.
4. True. The same also applies to lessee's separation of lease liabilities into current and long-term portions.
5. False. The advantages of a sale and leaseback accrue chiefly to the seller/lessee who can deduct more expense on the income tax return than would be possible if the leased property had *not* been sold and leased back, as long as a portion of the property is *not* a depreciable asset such as land.

If you missed any of the above questions, reread Frame 2[22] before proceeding. You have now completed Chapter 22. Go on to Chapter 23.

chapter 23

COMPARATIVE STATEMENTS AND RATIO ANALYSIS

Frame 1[23]

Statement of Accounting Policies and Auditors' Report

The financial analyst customarily begins by scrutinizing the footnotes detailing the accounting principles followed by the company. This provides a basis for assessing the performance and position of the company. For example, an analyst may be responsible for analyzing companies in a specific industry in which only one company uses straight-line depreciation. For that one company, the analyst may need to gather additional data to place all the companies on a comparable basis. Furthermore, unique industry-wide developments may make the financial statements of a particular year unrepresentative of all time periods in general. This may be explained in footnotes to the respective companies' financial statements. For reasons such as these it is imperative to give careful consideration to footnote disclosures.

It is also necessary to study the auditors' report on the company's financial statements, for this too may reveal unusual circumstances or unique developments of interest to the analyst. If an unusual item is deemed worthy of mention by the auditor, it is likely that investors and analysts will also be concerned about the item.

Comparative Statements

The financial statement for a company for one year gives a very limited view of the financial condition and profit potential; the long-run view is much more reliable. As a consequence, comparative financial statements, covering from two to ten years' operations are common. Likewise, single amounts on a financial statement, when viewed alone, generally have limited informational content and interpretative value. For example, a profit figure of $100,000 might look good at first sight, but it would appear far less favorable if the sales which generated it amounted to $100,000,000, that is, if profit was only one tenth of 1% of sales. Thus, there is a need for two kinds of analyses: (1) *horizontal analysis*—the comparison of amounts of one *period* with the amounts of another *period* (Illustration 23–1) and (2) vertical analysis—the comparison of one amount on the financial statement with another amount on that same statement (Illustration 23–2). In Illustration 23–1 (horizontal analysis) the comparison is in dollars; however, the differences also can be expressed as ratios or percentages. For example, the $1,000 increase in cash from $8,000 to $9,000 could be expressed as 12½% (that is, $1,000/$8,000). Vertical analyses are expressed as percentages, ratios, or other relative measurements, for obvious reasons.

Illustration 23–1

STANDARD MANUFACTURING COMPANY
Comparative Balance Sheets (Incomplete)
December 31, 19A and 19B

Assets	*December 31* *19B*	*19A*	*Increase Decrease** *19B over 19A*
Current Assets:			
Cash	$ 9,000	$ 8,000	$1,000
Notes receivable	1,000	2,000	1,000*
Accounts receivable	12,500	12,000	500
Total Receivables	13,500	14,000	500*
Less: Allowance for doubtful accounts	500	480	20
Net receivables	13,000	13,520	520*
Inventory	22,000	20,000	2,000
Prepaid insurance	200	300	100*
Total Current Assets	$44,200	$41,820	$2,380

Illustration 23–2

AUSTIN DRY GOODS STORE
Comparative Income Statements (Condensed)
For the Years Ended December 31, 19A, and 19B

	19B		*19A*	
	Amount	*Percent of Net Sales*	*Amount*	*Percent of Net Sales*
Gross sales	$151,500	101.0	$141,540	101.1
Less: Returns and allowances	1,500	1.0	1,540	1.1
Net sales	150,000	100.0	140,000	100.0
Cost of goods sold	105,000	70.0	99,400	71.0
Gross margin	45,000	30.0	40,600	29.0
Expenses:				
Selling expenses	7,500	5.0	7,560	5.4
General expenses	4,500	3.0	4,500	3.2
Financial expenses—net	750	.5	560	.4
Total Expenses	12,750	8.5	12,620	9.0
Net Income for Year	$ 32,250	21.5	$ 27,980	20.0

In computing percentages or ratios, one amount is selected as the *base amount* which becomes the divisor. For example, in Illustration 23–2 net sales is the base amount represented by 100%; consequently, it is divided into the other amounts to derive the respective percentages. In computing and interpreting percentage (or ratio) analyses, one must be aware of potentially misleading inferences when the amounts are relatively small; similarly, negative amounts should never be used. When there is no value for the base amount, relatives cannot be computed.

Ratio Analyses

A ratio is an expression of a relationship between two amounts; it may be expressed as a percentage, a decimal, or as a fraction. Thus, the relationship between, say, current assets of $200,000 and current liabilities of $100,000 could be expressed as 200%, 2.00 or 2 to 1. Ratio analysis is significant only when one amount bears a functional relationship to the other amount. Ratio analysis is a very important technique for interpreting financial data. The ratios presented in this chapter have received considerable attention because of their widespread usage. For any one company, however, the analyst may need to create additional ratios as analytical tools because of the company's unique situation. In analyzing financial statements there are three important groups of ratios:

1. Ratios indicating the current position.
2. Ratios indicating the equity position.
3. Ratios indicating profitability.

Ratios Indicating Current Position

The "current position" of a firm refers to its working capital position, that is, the relationship of current assets and current liabilities to each other and to other relevant values. The primary ratios providing an insight into current position are reviewed below:

Ratios Indicating Current Position

Ratio	*Formula for Computations*	*Significance*
Tests of overall solvency:		
1. Current ratio or working capital ratio.	Current assets (net) / Current liabilities	Primary test of solvency—indicates ability to meet current obligations from current assets as a going concern. Measure of adequacy of working capital.
2. Acid-test ratio or quick ratio.	Quick assets (net) / Current liabilities	A more severe test of immediate solvency than the current ratio. Tests ability to meet sudden demands upon current assets. (Quick assets is defined as current assets less inventories and prepaid expenses.)
3. Working capital to total assets.	Working capital / Total assets (net)	Indicates relative liquidity of total assets and distribution of resources employed. (Working capital is defined as current assets minus current liabilities.)
Ratios indicating movement of selected current assets (turnover):		
4. *a.* Receivable turnover.	Net credit sales / Average receivables (net)	Velocity of collection of trade accounts and notes. Test of efficiency of collection.
b. Age of receivables.	365 (days)* / Receivable turnover (computed per [*a*] above)	Average number of days to collect receivables.

5. Inventory turnover. *a.* Merchandise turnover (retail firm).	$\frac{\text{Cost of goods sold}}{\text{Average merchandise inventory}}$	Indicates liquidity of inventory. Number of times inventory turned over, or was sold, on the average during the period. Will exhibit tendency to over- or understock.
b. Finished goods turnover (manufacturing firm).	$\frac{\text{Cost of goods sold}}{\text{Average finished goods inventory}}$	Same as 5 (*a*).
c. Raw material turnover.	$\frac{\text{Cost of raw materials used}}{\text{Average raw materials inventory}}$	Number of times raw material inventory was used on the average during the period.
d. Days' supply in inventory.	$\frac{\text{365 (days)*}}{\text{Inventory turnover (computed per [a], [b], or [c] above)}}$	Number of days' supply in the average inventory for the year. Indicates general condition of over- or understocking as the case may be.
6. Working capital turnover.	$\frac{\text{Net sales}}{\text{Average working capital}}$	Indicates adequacy and activity of working capital.
7. Percent of each current asset to total current assets.	$\frac{\text{Each current asset}}{\text{Total current assets}}$	Indicates relative investment in each current asset.

* Some analysts prefer to use 360 days; others use 260 working days (i.e., 52 weeks × 5).

Ratios Indicating Equity Position

The right side of the balance sheet presents *two* basic sources of funds; that is, (1) the creditors' equity (total liabilities) and (2) owners' equity (total stockholders' equity). The following ratios are particularly relevant in assessing the equity position.

Ratios Indicating Equity Position

Ratio	*Formula for Computations*	*Significance*
Equity ratios:		
1. Owners' equity to total assets.	$\frac{\text{Owners' equity}}{\text{Total assets (net of depreciation)}}$	Proportion of assets provided by owners. Reflects financial strength and cushion for creditors.
2. Owners' equity to total liabilities.	$\frac{\text{Owners' equity}}{\text{Total liabilities}}$	Relative amounts of resources provided by owners and creditors. Reflects strengths and weaknesses in basic financing of operations.
3. Total liabilities to total assets.	$\frac{\text{Total liabilities}}{\text{Total assets (net of depreciation)}}$	Proportion of assets provided by creditors. Extent of "trading on the equity."
Equities related to profits and sales:		
4. Net income to owners' equity.	$\frac{\text{Net income}}{\text{Owners' equity}}$	Return on the resources provided by the owners.
5. Sales to owners' equity.	$\frac{\text{Sales (net)}}{\text{Owners' equity}}$	Number of times owners' equity is turned over in sales. Indicative of the utilization of owner capital. May suggest overcapitalization in relation to volume of business done.
Miscellaneous ratios related to equities:		
6. Fixed assets to fixed liabilities.	$\frac{\text{Fixed assets (net)}}{\text{Fixed liabilities}}$	Reflects extent of the utilization of resources from long-term debt. May suggest potential borrowing power. If the fixed assets are pledged—degree of security.
7. Fixed assets to owners' equity.	$\frac{\text{Fixed assets (net)}}{\text{Owners' equity}}$	Proportion of fixed assets to owners' equity. May suggest over- or underinvestment by owners. Also weakness or strength in "trading on the equity."

Ratio	Formula for Computation	Significance
8. Fixed assets to total equity.	Fixed assets (net) / Total liabilities and owners' equity	May suggest overexpansion of plant and equipment.
9. Sales to fixed assets (plant turnover).	Sales (net) / Fixed assets (net)	Turnover index which tests, roughly, the efficiency of management in keeping plant properties employed.
10. Book value per share of common stock.	Common stock equity / Number of outstanding shares	Number of dollars of equity (at book value) per share of common stock.

Determine whether each of the following statements is true or false.

_______ 1. Usually the quick ratio in most companies will be equal to, or less than, the current ratio.

_______ 2. When credit terms are n/30, the approximate expected receivable turnover rate is 12 times a year.

_______ 3. Assume a company reports a negative (deficit) total for stockholders' equity. The ratio of total liabilities to total assets will be greater than 1 to 1; for example, 1.5 to 1.

_______ 4. Assume a company purchased treasury stock at a cost in excess of its book value, then immediately retired it. The effect would be to decrease book value per share (for the remaining shares).

Now check your responses by comparing them with Answer Frame 1[23], page 100.

Frame 2[23]

Ratios Indicating Profitability

The success of a firm is measured more in terms of its *profit-making potential* and *growth* than in the total sum of the assets controlled. In the final analysis, in a competitive capitalistic economy, the overall measure of managerial success (or failure) is profitability. Unfortunately, profitability is not susceptible to adequate measurement in only *one* amount such as dollar profits, percentage of profits to sales, etc. Profitability fundamentally relates to *return on the investment,* whereas growth primarily relates to increases over time in sales, profits, and return on investment. The primary ratios that measure profitability are reviewed below.

Ratios Indicating Profitability

Ratio	*Formula for Computation*	*Significance*
1. Net income to net sales (profit margin).	Net income / Net sales	Indicates net productivity of each dollar of sales.
2. Net income to owners' equity.	Net income / Average owners' equity	Earnings rate on resources provided by owners.
3. Investment turnover.	Net sales / Total investment	Number of times total investment (total assets) turns. Indicative of efficiency with which total resources are utilized.
4. Net income earned per share of common stock.	Net income minus preferred dividend requirements / Average number of shares of common stock outstanding	Profit earned on each share of common stock. Indicative of ability to pay dividends.

5. Earnings rate on market value per share.	$\frac{\text{Net income per share}}{\text{Market price per share}}$	Earnings rate based on current market price per share of stock. Indicates profitability of firm related to market value of stockholders' equity.
6. Price-earnings ratio.	$\frac{\text{Market price per share}}{\text{Net income per share}}$	Another way to express the relationship in 5 above.
7. Return on investment (return on assets employed).	$\frac{\text{Net income plus interest expense*}}{\text{Total assets}}$	Represents rate earned by management on all resources committed to the firm. Indicates ability of management to conduct profitable operations.

* Net of tax.

Return on Investment

Listed among the ratios indicating *profitability* was return on investment (ROI). This ratio has considerable relevance, since it is the only ratio that combines the effect of the *three major factors* in *profitability:* (1) sales revenue, (2) profit, and (3) investment. Return on investment may be derived by the computation of net income divided by investment. However, it assumes more meaning when viewed as the product of two other ratios, the profit margin and the investment turnover (page 98). To illustrate, assume the following data:

Sales	$200,000
Net income . . .	20,000
Total assets . . .	100,000

Computation of the ratios:

1. $\frac{\text{Income}}{\text{Sales}} = \frac{\$20,000}{\$200,000} = 10\%$ (profit margin)

2. $\frac{\text{Sales}}{\text{Total assets}} = \frac{\$200,000}{\$100,000} = 2$ (investment turnover)

3. 10% (profit margin) × 2 (investment turnover) = 20% return on investment

Or

$\frac{\text{Income}}{\text{Total assets}} = \frac{\$20,000}{\$100,000} = 20\%$ return on total investment (total assets employed)

In computing return on investment one must carefully define both "net income" and "investment," since there are a number of different methods of computing any of the ratios reviewed in this chapter. Net income can be defined variously for this purpose, such as "pretax," "before extraordinary items," "before interest expense," "before depreciation," and so on. Similarly, investment can be defined in ways such as "total liabilities plus total capital," "total capital," "total tangible capital," and so on. Perhaps the most common computation of ROI is "net income after tax, before extraordinary items, and before deduction of interest expense" divided by "total liabilities plus total capital." Interest expense is not deducted from net income in this instance, since it is part of the return on *total* assets, those financed with debt and those financed with stockholder's equity.

A slightly different set of ROI ratios indicates the impact on the company's ROI from financing part of their operations with debt and is known as the leverage factor, or "trading on the equity." Investors who loan money to corporations expect less return than investors in the stock of the corporation because the corporation is obligated to pay to creditors interest plus the principal amount of the loan at maturity. Consequently, they assume less risk than investors in stock. Corporations are therefore able to reduce their "cost of capital" by financing a part of their operations with debt.

Answer frame 1[23]

1. True. The quick ratio and the current ratio are different only because of the different items included in the numerator. The numerator usually will be less for the quick ratio than for the current ratio because of inventories and prepaid expenses.
2. True. The approximate expectation would be that the receivables, on the average, would be paid in 30 days, therefore the expected turnover would be:

$$\frac{\text{Net credit sales}}{\text{Average receivables}} = \frac{\text{365 days of sales}}{\text{30 days of sales}} = 12.16 \text{ times per year}$$

3. True. When total liabilities (the numerator) is greater than the denominator, the ratio between them obviously would be greater than 1 to 1 (i.e., there are fewer total assets than total liabilities).
4. True. The total amount of stockholders' equity decreases by a greater relative amount than the total number of shares remaining as outstanding; consequently, book value per share will decrease.

If you missed any of the above questions, reread Frame 1[23] before proceeding. Then turn to Frame 2[23], page 98, and continue reading.

Frame 2[23] continued

To illustrate, assume the following data:

Net income	$ 20,000
Interest expense	1,000
Owners' equity	60,000
Total assets	100,000
Income tax rate	40%

1. Return on owners' equity measures the return to investors in stock only:

$$\frac{\text{Net income}}{\text{Owners' equity}} = \frac{\$20,000}{\$60,000} = 33.3\%$$

2. Return on total investment measures the return on total assets including that portion financed by creditors. For this reason, the interest expense, net of tax, must be added back to net income (because it was deducted in arriving at net income).

$$\frac{\text{Net income + Interest expense, net of tax}}{\text{Total assets}} = \frac{\$20,000 + \$1,000(.60)}{\$100,000} = \frac{\$20,600}{\$100,000} = 20.6\%$$

3. The financial leverage factor is the difference between the two ROI numbers.

$$33.3\% - 20.6\% = 12.7\%$$

In this case, the investors in stock are benefited by the corporation's debt financing.

Utilization of Ratio Analyses

Ratio analysis should be considered as a supplementary technique to be used in the interpretation of financial statements. Ratios should be selected that are relevant to the kind of decision that is under consideration. There are a number of fairly standard ratios, such as those reviewed above; however, their manner of detailed computation is not standardized. Ratios tend to reflect average conditions and are no better than the quality of the data used to compute them. Changes in the accounting system and classifications may affect a particular ratio. One ratio standing alone seldom has much significance; rather, a number of ratios and the trends reflected in them over several periods of time may provide a reliable reading. It is suggested that in evaluating the ratios for the period under consideration they be compared with:

1. Those of preceding periods for the company.
2. Those of leading competitors.
3. Those of the industry (average) in which the company operates.
4. Budgeted and standard ratios developed by the company as goals.

Finally, it should be mentioned that most of the ratios illustrated in this chapter utilized book values for such items as total assets and owners' equity. In most cases, added meaning can be given to the ratios by using market values instead.

Determine whether each of the following statements is true or false.

_______ 1. Basically, earnings per share is computed by dividing net income for the period by the total number of shares issued.

_______ 2. A 10 to 1 price-earnings ratio implies a per share earnings rate on the market price of 1 to 10.

_______ 3. In general, one would expect the return on total assets to exceed the return on owners' equity.

_______ 4. As net income per share of stock increases, book value per share of stock increases, other things held constant.

Now check your responses by referring to Answer Frame 2[23], page 102.

Answer frame 2[23]

1. False. Basically, earnings per share is computed by dividing net income for the period by the number of shares *outstanding*. Some of the shares issued could now be held as treasury stock or could have been canceled.
2. True. The price-earnings ratio and the earnings-price ratio are reciprocals; that is, the two variables used are the same, only the computations are inverted.
3. False. Return on total assets includes the company's return on assets financed by debt as well as the return on assets financed by stock. Return on owners' equity includes only the return on assets financed with stock. Because the return on stock is normally higher than the return on debt, the return on owners' equity normally exceeds the return on total assets.
4. True. Net income increases book value. Therefore, if other factors are held constant, higher net income implies higher book value.

If you missed any of the above, reread Frame 2[23] before you go on to Chapter 24.

chapter 24

THE GENERAL PURCHASING POWER (GPP) ACCOUNTING MODEL

Frame 1[24]

Effects of Changes in the Value of the Measuring Unit

The period since World War II has been characterized by steady inflation, with prices escalating significantly during 1974–75. Thus, the assumption that the purchasing power of the dollar is stable over time is demonstrably false. This of course causes one to question the validity of the historical cost accounting model. The concern is justified, and, accordingly, the discussion that follows covers one alternative that has been proposed to the historical cost model. Chapter 25 will cover two other alternative models that have also been proposed. First, however, we will consider the effect *inflation* has on historical cost financial statements. The discussion would be perfectly general if we considered price deflation as well as inflation. But because *inflation* is more common, we will limit the discussion, examples, and so forth, to the latter.

The test of any model (or any theory) is the quality of the descriptions (or the predictions) that the model generates. That is, a model is useful if it produces valid descriptions, even if the underlying assumptions of the model are not strictly met. Accountants have long been aware of the changing purchasing power of the dollar. However, the need to consider alternative accounting models has not been critical because until recently prices advanced at a manageable rate, and as a result the historical cost model has, in general, produced useful accounting numbers. Since 1974, however, the rate of inflation has caused accountants and other business people to reexamine the validity of the historical cost framework.

The negative ramifications of *inflation* result from the fact that very high rates of *inflation* erode the quality of decisions that are based solely on historical cost numbers. That is, *ignoring* inflation is bad. For example, assume a company acquired a building in 1960 at a cost of $100,000. Over the next 17 years, prices rose dramatically, and in 1978 the same building would cost $175,000 to replace in kind. If this company had priced its products to cover only the historical cost depreciation of $5,000 per year, it would probably be unable to replace the building in 1980 without financing a substantial portion of the higher acquisition cost with debt. On the other hand, if the company had made some ad hoc adjustments to its pricing policies, it would have had a better chance to finance the replacement with internally generated funds. The subject matter of this chapter is a *systematic framework* for considering the effects of inflation on financial statements. The framework, or alternative accounting model, is referred to as the *general purchasing power* (referred to hereafter as *GPP*) or the price-level accounting model.

Overview of the GPP Model

The GPP model explicitly considers the effect of inflation by restating all account balances in terms of dollars with equivalent purchasing power. In this manner, the cost of fixed asests acquired in 1960, items of inventory acquired late in 1977, and capital stock issued in 1945 are all stated in common dollars. The vehicle for restating account balances is a price-level index ratio which utilizes some index of general purchasing power, such as the Gross National Product Implicit Price Deflator (GNP Deflator) or the Consumer Price Index. It is generally agreed that it is most useful to restate balances into dollars of *current* purchasing power. For example, assume that the building referred to above was acquired for $100,000 when the price index stood at 120. It is now 18 years later and the current price index is 180. The cost of this building would be reported on a GPP balance sheet at $150,000, or $100,000 × (180/120) = $150,000. The GPP-adjusted cost of $150,000 may or may not equal the current market value of the building. Thus, GPP accounting is not market value accounting. In fact, the GPP model maintains historical cost amounts—but adjusted for the general change in the purchasing power of the dollar.

In December 1974 the Financial Accounting Standards Board (FASB) issued an exposure draft on GPP accounting. Since that time the FASB has *not* issued a formal statement requiring companies to prepare and publicly issue GPP financial statements. At the date of this writing, the historical cost model is the generally accepted accounting model. However, in 1976, the Securities and Exchange Commission (SEC) began requiring companies to disclose limited *current replacement cost* data as supplements to the historical cost financial statements. It seems obvious that the FASB's not moving ahead to implement the GPP model has been affected by the SEC's replacement cost disclosure requirement. Nevertheless, because the GPP model is a viable alternative to the historical cost model, and because the FASB's exposure draft reflects current thinking on GPP accounting, the material which follows reflects the position proposed in the exposure draft.

Four distinct features of the FASB version of the GPP model are:

1. The *GNP Deflator* is recommended as the price index because it is the most general price index available. The GNP Deflator includes all items used to calculate gross national product.
2. Restate account balances in terms of *current dollars*. One alternative would be to restate account balances in terms of 1958 dollars. The GNP Deflator for 1958 was 100.
3. Use an *average price index* value to restate revenues and expenses that occur rather evenly over an accounting period. The alternative is to GPP adjust every transaction, which is generally not feasible.
4. Report the *GPP gain or loss* (from holding monetary items) as a separate item on the *income statement*. The alternative is to report the GPP gain or loss as a separate element of stockholders' equity on the balance sheet. This item will be explained more fully below.

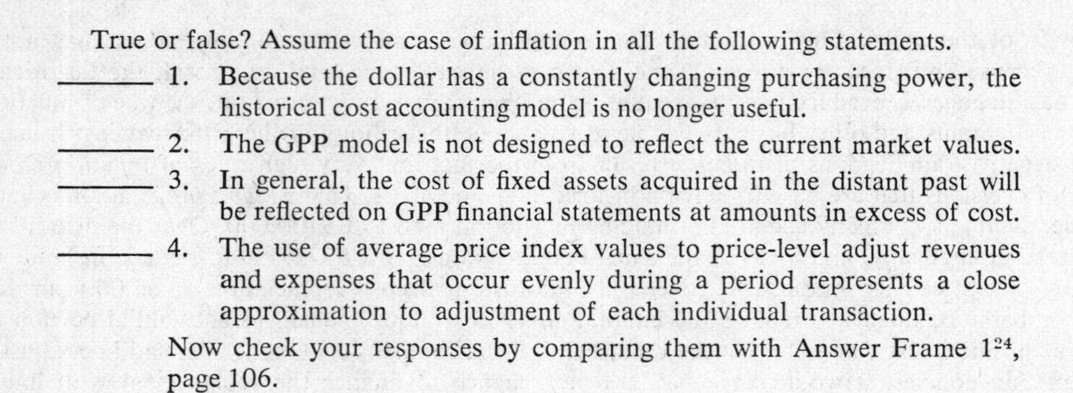
True or false? Assume the case of inflation in all the following statements.

_______ 1. Because the dollar has a constantly changing purchasing power, the historical cost accounting model is no longer useful.

_______ 2. The GPP model is not designed to reflect the current market values.

_______ 3. In general, the cost of fixed assets acquired in the distant past will be reflected on GPP financial statements at amounts in excess of cost.

_______ 4. The use of average price index values to price-level adjust revenues and expenses that occur evenly during a period represents a close approximation to adjustment of each individual transaction.

Now check your responses by comparing them with Answer Frame 1[24], page 106.

Frame 2[24]

Monetary and Nonmonetary Items

The distinction between *monetary* and *nonmonetary* items is important in the GPP model for purposes of computing the *GPP gain or loss* for the period. A simple illustration will make this clear. Assume that ABC Corporation began operations with $10,000 cash. The corporation considered two alternative uses of the cash. Alternative 1 was to invest in a 6% savings deposit at a bank. Alternative 2 was to purchase a high-quality stock in another corporation that has consistently paid a cash dividend at the rate of $600 per $10,000 of market value of its stock. During ABC's first year of operation, *all prices* in the economy rose by 6%. If ABC had invested in either the savings account or the stock, the 6% earnings would have kept pace with inflation. If the corporation had chosen to withdraw its deposit from the bank at year-end, it would have received exactly $10,000. But if the corporation had chosen to sell the stock at year-end, it would have realized proceeds of $10,600, the cost plus the 6% rise in price (assuming the fair market value of the stock increased at the same rate as inflation). In this case the investor would have fared better by buying the stock than by depositing his cash in the savings account.

The above illustration is a gross generalization of existing facts, but it illustrates that:

1. *Monetary* items such as the savings deposit are stated in a *fixed* number of dollars that *do not change* as prices change. Therefore, one who holds *net monetary assets* (monetary assets in excess of monetary liabilities) *loses* purchasing power during inflation. One who holds *net monetary liabilities gains* purchasing power during inflation because the debt is repaid with cheaper dollars than borrowed (and supposedly invested).
2. *Nonmonetary* items such as the stock in the example (or plant, equipment, and land) are stated in a number of dollars that *can change* as prices change. Therefore one who holds only *nonmonetary* items can have *neither* GPP gain nor GPP loss because the value of the holdings are assumed to keep pace with inflation.

On the basis of the above distinction, GPP gains or losses are computed on monetary items only.

A fairly complete listing of monetary and nonmonetary items is given below:

Monetary items:

Cash
Marketable securities—bonds to be held to maturity
Accounts receivable
Allowance for bad debts
Notes receivable
Most other receivables

Cash surrender value of life insurance
Investments in bonds—to be held to maturity

Accounts payable
Notes payable
Cash dividends payable
Bonds payable
Unamortized premium or discount on bonds payable
Convertible bonds payable—until converted
Preferred stockholders' equity—if stated at liquidation value

Nonmonetary items:
Cash in foreign currency
Marketable securities—stocks; bonds to be converted to cash before maturity
Merchandise inventory
Prepaid expenses
Investments in bonds—to be converted to cash before maturity
Property, plant, and equipment
Accumulated depreciation
Intangible assets (patents, trademarks, goodwill, etc.)
Deferred tax expense

Deferred (unearned) income
Obligations under warranties
Deferred tax liabilities
Common stockholders' equity
Preferred stockholders' equity—if *not* stated at liquidation value

Without referring to the list of monetary and nonmonetary items, answer the following true/false questions. Assume prices are rising (i.e., inflation).

______ 1. A firm that has one asset, cash, and one liability, a note payable, and no owners' equity will have neither a GPP gain nor a GPP loss.

______ 2. Monetary assets entitle the owner to receive a specified number of dollars.

______ 3. All liabilities are monetary items.

______ 4. A short-term investment in bonds with several years to maturity will give rise to a GPP loss because the bond investment entitles the owner to receive a specified number of dollars.

Now check your responses by comparing them with Answer Frame 2[24], page 106.

Frame 3[24]

A Comprehensive Illustration

The foregoing theoretical material will now be incorporated into an illustration of the mechanics of implementing the GPP model. It is helpful to proceed by applying the following steps:

1. *Separate* the balance sheet into *monetary* and *nonmonetary* items.
2. Compute the *GPP gain or loss* for the period.

Answer frame 1[24]

1. False. Despite its shortcomings, the historical cost model is useful because it provides objective data. Users with different decision models can alter the historical cost numbers to suit their own needs. Furthermore, as long as price changes are not dramatic and assets have relatively short lives, historical cost numbers approximate current market values.
2. True. The GPP model reflects price-level adjusted historical cost, but *not necessarily* what each asset would sell for at the current date.
3. True. During inflation, as long as account balances are restated in terms of current dollars, assets will be restated into more dollars than the assets cost when they were acquired. However, each of the current dollars has less purchasing power than did each of the older dollars. Therefore, it takes more current dollars to purchase the same service potential acquired earlier, given inflation.
4. True. The average price index for the period captures the essence of the period's price movements. Therefore, as long as the revenue or expense involved assets or liabilities that were affected evenly during the period, use of the average price index for restatement will closely approximate the aggregate of all the individually price-level adjusted revenue or expense transactions.

If you missed any of the above, restudy Frame 1[24] before turning to Frame 2[24] on page 104.

Answer frame 2[24]

1. True. The firm has only monetary items, which, in general, produce GPP gains or losses. In this case, however, the firm has a monetary asset and a monetary liability, so the loss on the asset is offset by the gain on the liability.
2. True. This is the definition of a monetary asset.
3. False. Unearned revenues are liabilities the satisfaction of which requires of the debtor asset outlays such as labor cost, merchandise inventory, supplies, or other items that can take on different values during inflation. In this respect unearned revenues are distinguished from accounts or notes payable, which require of the debtor asset outlays that are stated in a fixed number of dollars.
4. False. A short-term investment in bonds is classified as a marketable security because it is expected to be converted to cash within the company's operating cycle, which usually precedes the maturity date of the bonds. Therefore, the sale of the bonds can be expected to generate cash proceeds that are not fixed in amount. For this reason, this investment is a nonmonetary item and as such it does not give rise to a GPP gain or loss.

If you missed any of the above questions, reread Frame 2[24] before proceeding to Frame 3[24], page 105. Then continue reading.

Frame 3[24] continued

3. Prepare the *GPP income statement* for the period, including the GPP gain or loss.
4. Prepare the *GPP balance sheet* as of the end of the period.

Assume that L Corporation performs a service and therefore earns Service Revenue. Illustration 24–1 gives L Corporation's balance sheets, stated at historical cost, as of December 31, 19C, and December 31, 19D, as well as other data needed to make the GPP adjustments.

Illustration 24–1

L CORPORATION
Balance Sheet—Historical Cost
December 31, 19C, and 19D

Assets		19C		19D
Cash		$150		$200
Machinery	$400		$500	
Less: Accumulated depreciation	(100)	300	(150)	350
Total Assets		$450		$550
Liabilities				
Accounts payable		$100		$150
Owners' Equity				
Stock, other contributed capital, and retained earnings		350		400
		$450		$550

Additional data:

1. Machinery was purchased for $400 cash on July 1, 19A. All machines have ten-year lives, and straight-line depreciation is used with a zero salvage value.
2. Transactions for 19D include:

Date	*Nature*	*Amount*
January 1, 19D	Purchased machinery for cash	$100
July 1, 19D	Purchased supplies on account	150
Even through 19D	Received cash for services performed	600
Even through 19D	Paid wages	300
Even through 19D	Used supplies	150
Even through 19D	Depreciation expense	50
Even through 19D	Paid income tax	50
October 1, 19D	Paid on account	100

3. Index numbers of the general price index:

Date	*Index Number*	
July 1, 19A	87	
December 31, 19C	106	
January 1, 19D	106	Average for 19D = 108.2
April 1, 19D	105	
July 1, 19D	109	
October 1, 19D	109	
December 31, 19D	112	

Now we can produce GPP-adjusted financial statements by applying the four steps mentioned above.

Step 1—Monetary items are Cash and Accounts Payable. All other balance sheet accounts are non-monetary.

Step 2—Computation of GPP gain or loss.

The logic involved in the computation of GPP gain or loss deserves some explanation. First, beginning net monetary assets need to be restated into dollars that have the same purchasing power as dollars at year-end, when the price index is 112. An implicit assumption involved in this illustrative restatement is that both beginning cash and beginning accounts payable, the components of net monetary assets in this illustration, arose on January 1, 19D.

Illustration 24–2

L CORPORATION
Computation of GPP Gain or Loss
Year Ended December 31, 19D

	Historical	*GPP Conversion Ratio*	*GPP Adjusted*
Net monetary assets (cash less accounts payable) at December 31, 19C .	$ 50	112/106	$ 52.83
Additions to net monetary assets during 19D:			
Cash sales	600	112/108.2	621.07
Reductions in net monetary assets during 19D:			
Purchased machinery with cash	(100)	112/106	(105.66)
Purchased supplies on account	(150)	112/109	(154.13)
Paid wages	(300)	112/108.2	(310.54)
Paid income taxes	(50)	112/108.2	(51.75)
Net monetary assets, *historical* at December 31, 19D	$ 50		
Net monetary assets, *GPP adjusted* at December 31, 19D			$ 51.82
Less: Net monetary asset, *historical* at December 31, 19D			(50.00)
GPP loss on monetary items for 19D			$ 1.82

Second, restate in terms of year-end dollars all 19D transactions that affected (any component of) net monetary assets. It is worth noting that the *purchase* of supplies, which created the account payable (a monetary item) and *not* the *use* of the supplies, affected *net monetary* items. Also, the October 1 payment of the account payable had no effect on GPP gain or loss because the net effect of this transaction (Dr. Accounts Payable, Cr. Cash) on net monetary items is zero.

The third, and final, step in the GPP gain or loss computation is to arrive at net monetary assets at year-end and then to subtract the historical balance from the GPP-adjusted balance. A negative result constitutes a GPP gain, and a positive result constitutes a GPP loss. In Illustration 24–2, the resulting nonnegative difference of $1.82 is labeled a loss. The substance of the comparison and the related logic are as follows: L Corporation transacted business during 19D in such a way as to have net monetary assets with a purchasing power of $51.82 at year-end. However, L Corporation actually had only $50 in net monetary assets at that time. The resulting difference of $1.82 thus constitutes a GPP loss for the year. Application of this same logic dictates that a negative difference is a GPP gain for the period.

Step 3—Income statement—GPP adjusted:

Illustration 24–3

L CORPORATION
Income Statement—GPP Adjusted
Year Ended December 31, 19D

	Historical		*GPP Conversion Ratio*	*GPP Adjusted*	
Service revenue		$600	112/108.2		$621.07
Expenses:					
Wages	$300		112/108.2	$310.54	
Supplies	150		112/109	154.13	
Depreciation—machinery	40		112/87	51.49	
	10		112/106	10.57	
Income taxes	50		112/108.2	51.75	
GPP loss				1.82	
Total Expenses		550			580.30
Net Income, Historical		$ 50			
Net Income, GPP Adjusted					$ 40.77

Step 4—Balance sheet—GPP adjusted:

Illustration 24–4

L CORPORATION
Balance Sheet—GPP Adjusted
December 31, 19D

Assets	*Historical*			*GPP Conversion Ratio*		*GPP Adjusted*	
Cash			$200				$200.00
Machinery	$400			112/87	$514.94		
	100	$500		112/106	105.66	$620.60	
Less: Accumulated depreciation	140			112/87	180.23		
	10	150	350	112/106	10.57	190.80	429.80
Total Assets			$550				$629.80
Liabilities							
Accounts payable			$150				$150.00
Owners' Equity							
Stock, other contributed capital, and retained earnings			400				479.80*
Total Equities			$550				$629.80

* This is a balancing figure; that is, $629.80 − $150.00 = $479.80.

The GPP-adjusted income statement is self-explanatory. Three items on the GPP-adjusted balance sheet, however, need to be clarified. The first two are the monetary items (cash and accounts payable) which are not price-level adjusted because they are monetary items (refer once again to the definition of monetary items given on page 104).

The third item is stockholders' equity, which is typically separated into its component parts in historical cost financial statements in order to satisfy legal requirements pertaining to dividends, and so on. Because those legal requirements are stated in terms of historical cost amounts, the GPP-adjusted amounts for stock, other contributed capital, and retained earnings have little meaning. For this reason, they may be combined into one stockholders' equity amount for the GPP-adjusted balance sheet.

Also, note that the stockholders' equity amount, $479.80, is a balancing figure. There is a way, however, to test the accuracy of the GPP-adjusted balance of stockholders' equity. Briefly stated, the test involves (1) "rolling forward" (i.e., price-level adjusting) all items (including monetary items) on the beginning balance sheet except beginning stockholders' equity. Thus, the GPP-adjusted beginning stockholders' equity amount is a balancing figure. Then (2) the GPP-adjusted net income from the income statement is added to the GPP-adjusted *beginning* stockholders' equity to arrive at GPP-adjusted *ending* stockholders' equity. This amount should equal the ending balancing figure, such as the $479.80 which was obtained in Illustration 24–4.

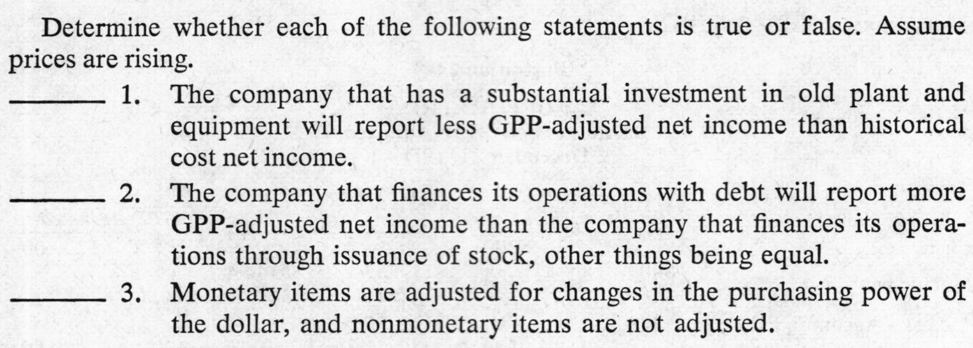

Determine whether each of the following statements is true or false. Assume prices are rising.

______ 1. The company that has a substantial investment in old plant and equipment will report less GPP-adjusted net income than historical cost net income.

______ 2. The company that finances its operations with debt will report more GPP-adjusted net income than the company that finances its operations through issuance of stock, other things being equal.

______ 3. Monetary items are adjusted for changes in the purchasing power of the dollar, and nonmonetary items are not adjusted.

Work the following problem.

4. On June 30, 19A (price index = 175), Q, Inc., had as its only asset $5,000 in cash. On the same day, Q, Inc., spent the cash to acquire a machine for $5,000. The machine is being depreciated over five years on the straight-line method with an estimated residual value of $500 (stated in June 30, 19A, dollars). On September 30, 19C (price index = 210), Q, Inc., purchased merchandise inventory on account for $1,000. These are the only transactions Q, Inc., entered into from June 30, 19A, until January 1, 19D. At December 31, 19C (price index = 212), Q, Inc., will report total assets, adjusted for GPP and stated in terms of December 31, 19C, dollars of ______.

Now check your responses against those for Answer Frame 3[24] given on page 112.

chapter 25

CURRENT REPLACEMENT COST AND MARKET VALUE MODELS

Frame 1[25]

Chapters 1–23 of this series cover the historical cost accounting model. Chapter 24 covers the general purchasing power model. The early discussion in Chapter 24 is quite general, however, in that it pertains to the general class of problems inherent in the historical cost model during periods of inflation (and deflation). From that point of departure, Chapter 24 presents a supplementary extension of the historical cost model. That extension requires only a restatement of the historically determined account balances. The present chapter covers two full-blown alternatives to the historical cost model, each of which represents a significant departure therefrom.

Current Replacement Cost (CRC) Accounting[1]

Business entities can earn income from two types of activities: (1) *operating* activities and (2) *holding* activities. The former relates to converting inputs such as materials, labor, and so on, into products of output, whereas the latter relates to holding assets that rise or fall in value. One of the most severe criticisms of the historical cost model is that it does *not* separate the two types of income. For example, a company may purchase a machine to be used in manufacturing its product. After one year, the cost of a comparable machine may have risen dramatically even though the newer machine has no technological advantage over the firm's one-year-old machine. In this case, the firm has a competitive advantage over competing firms that must pay the higher price for the newer, albeit comparable machine. This firm, therefore, has a *cost savings* (associated with its holding the machine) that the historical cost model ignores.

Another, more important criticism of the historical cost model has to do with reporting operating results during periods of inflation. The criticism, which was alluded to in Chapter 24, is that under the historical cost model, expenses (such as depreciation) associated with long-lived assets are not adequate to shelter sufficient resources to provide for replacement of the assets when they expire. The general purchasing power (GPP) model addresses this problem by a systematic process of restating depreciation (and other) expenses in terms of current units of general purchasing power. This technique is suboptimal, however, to the extent that the replacement cost of equivalent assets are not accurately reflected in the GPP-adjusted depreciation expense.

To remedy this problem, proponents of *current replacement cost* (*CRC*) accounting favor matching expenses based on the *unique* current replacement cost of the operating assets against the revenue of the period. In this way, it is asserted that the difference (i.e., operating income) is a better measure of current operations than the historical cost operating income which represents current revenue less historical

[1] The discussion of CRC accounting is largely adapted from Edgar O. Edwards and Phillip Bell, *The Theory and Measurement of Business Income* published in 1967 by the University of California Press.

Answer frame 3[24]

1. True *or* false. Answer depends on other factors in addition to age of plant and equipment. One critical factor is the manner by which fixed asset acquisitions were financed. If they were financed with debt, then the net effects of inflation may leave the firm's GPP-adjusted net income equal to its historical cost net income.
2. True. The debt-financed company will report GPP gains on its liabilities. This is one weakness of the GPP model, for empirically there seems to be some maximum viable amount of debt in each company's financing mix. Unfortunately the GPP model does not give effect to this basic fact.
3. False. Monetary items are not adjusted; nonmonetary items are adjusted.
4. $4,341. Computations:

	Machine		*Inventory*		*Total Assets*
Cost	$5,000		$1,000		
Less residual value	(500)				
Depreciable cost	4,500				
÷ Estimated life—years	÷ 5				
Depreciation per year	900				
June 30, 19A–December 31, 19C	× 2½				
Accumulated depreciation at December 31, 19C	2,250				
Book value	2,750		1,000		
GPP conversion ratio	(212/175)		(212/210)		
GPP adjusted book value	$3,331	+	$1,010	=	$4,341

If you missed any of the above, reread Frame 3[24] before proceeding. You have now completed Chapter 24. Continue reading with Chapter 25 on page 111.

Frame 1[25] continued

cost, or the GPP-adjusted income (which implicitly assumes that all prices move exactly together). Thus, CRC-derived operating income is believed to better reflect the firm's success in converting inputs (at current cost) into outputs (which are already stated at current prices). It is generally agreed that companies must earn sufficient operating income to replace a target portion of their worn-out assets in order to remain viable over the long run. This brief description of the CRC model suggests that one of the basic intents of the model is to facilitate the *preservation of capital.*

The CRC model can be modified to separate the elements of cost savings that are due to (1) rises in the general index of prices (i.e., *general* price-level changes) and (2) price increases that are unique to the particular asset in question (i.e., *specific* price changes). To illustrate, assume that a company acquired a machine at a cost of $10,000 when the general price index stood at 100. One year later, the same machine cost $12,500 and the price index value was 115. In this case the cost saving on the machine, ignoring depreciation, was $2,500, and of this total cost saving, we may label $1,500 (i.e., ($10,000 × 115/100) − $10,000 = $1,500) of it as *fictional* because all prices, in general, rose by 15%. The additional $1,000 (i.e., $2,500 − $1,500 = $1,000) of cost saving may be labeled as *real* because it exceeded the general increase in prices and hence was unique to the machine.

In a fashion similar to the separation of real and fictional elements of cost saving, *realized* and *unrealized* cost savings can also be separated. Refer once again to the example in the preceding paragraph, and assume that the annual depreciation rate on the machine is 20%. At the end of the first year, 20% of the cost saving of $2,500, or $500, is *realized* through use of the machine, and the remaining 80%, or $2,000, is *unrealized,* awaiting usage of the asset in the future. And it is also possible to separate the realized and unrealized cost savings into real and fictional elements, as follows:

	Cost Savings				
	Real		*Fictional*		*Totals*
Realized . . .	.20 ($1,000) =	$ 200	.20 ($1,500) =	$ 300	$ 500
Unrealized . .	.80 ($1,000) =	800	.80 ($1,500) =	1,200	2,000
Totals .		$1,000		$1,500	$2,500

The CRC model is rather flexible inasmuch as the various elements of cost savings can be presented in the financial statements in a number of different ways. *One approach,* which is consistent with the realization principle of the traditional accounting model, is to report *realized* cost savings on the *income statement* and *unrealized* cost savings on the *balance sheet. Another approach,* and the one favored by the authors, is to report *real* cost savings, both *realized and unrealized,* on the *income statement* and all *fictional* elements of cost savings in the stockholders' equity section of the *balance sheet.* Finally, it should be noted that the CRC accounting model builds upon the historical cost account balances, which may be used for computing taxes and for other purposes.

Illustration of CRC Entries and Financial Statements

Now a very simple example will illustrate the entries and financial statements that the CRC accounting system described above could be expected to produce. The reader should be aware that this is only one of a number of current replacement cost accounting models that have been proposed in the literature, and at the date of this writing none of them can be classified as GAAP. But this model includes the basic elements that are common to most of the other models as well.

In the illustration that follows, we shall assume that it is appropriate to report all *real* cost savings on the *income statement* and all *fictional* cost savings on the *balance sheet.* Furthermore, the entity in question, which we shall name Corporation, is service oriented. This will avoid the complexities that arise from the different inventory costing methods. Illustration 25–1 presents Corporation's balance sheet as of December 31, 19A, its income statement for the year ended December 31, 19B, and its December 31, 19B, balance sheet, all on a historical cost basis. The illustration also presents some additional information needed for the CRC adjustments.

Illustration 25–2 gives the historical cost journal entries that were made to produce the 19B income

Illustration 25–1

CORPORATION
Balance Sheet
December 31, 19A

Cash	$100
Accounts receivable	200
Fixed asset . . .	500
Less: Accumulated depreciation	(100)
	$700
Liabilities	$300
Owners' equity . .	400
	$700

CORPORATION
Income Statement
Year Ended
December 31, 19B

Service revenue		$700
Expenses:		
Depreciation .	$100	
Other . . .	400	500
Net Income . .		$200

CORPORATION
Balance Sheet
December 31, 19B

Cash	$ 350
Accounts receivable	350
Fixed asset . . .	500
Less: Accumulated depreciation	(200)
	$1,000
Liabilities	$ 400
Owners' equity . .	600
	$1,000

Additional data:

1. Price index values: December 31, 19A, 100; average for 19B, 110.
2. Services rendered and other expenses occurred evenly during 19B.
3. Average current replacement cost of fixed asset during 19B was $575.
4. Annual depreciation rate on fixed asset is 20%.

statement and 19B year-end balance sheet above. It also presents in comparative form the related current replacement cost entries.

Illustration 25–2

Historical Cost Entries			*CRC Entries*		
1. To record realization of service revenue (one entry for all 19B revenues):					
Accounts receivable	700		Accounts receivable	700	
Service revenue		700	Service revenue		700
2. To collect accounts receivable (one entry for 19B's total collections):					
Cash	550		Cash	550	
Accounts receivable		550	Accounts receivable		550
3. To recognize other expenses (one entry for all 19B other expenses):					
Expenses	400		Expenses	400	
Cash		300	Cash		300
Liabilities		100	Liabilities		100
4. To write fixed assets up to current replacement cost:					
No entry			Fixed asset—unrealized cost savings, real	25	
			Fixed asset—unrealized cost savings, fictional	50	
			Unrealized cost saving, real		25
			Unrealized cost saving, fictional		50

Computations:

Total cost saving ($575 − $500)	$75
Less: Fictional cost saving ($500 × 110/100 − $500)	50
Real cost saving	$25

The *fixed-asset—cost savings* accounts are balance sheet valuation accounts, and, given our assumption as to the manner of reporting (credit balance) *cost savings* accounts, the *real* cost saving is to be reported on the *income statement*, whereas the *fictional* cost saving account is to be reported as an element of *owners' equity*.

Historical Cost Entries			*CRC Entries*		
5. To record depreciation expense for 19B:					
Depreciation expense	100		Depreciation expense	115	
Accumulated depreciation		100	Accumulated depreciation		100
			Accumulated depreciation—fixed asset—unrealized cost saving, real		5
			Accumulated depreciation—fixed asset—unrealized cost saving, fictional		10

Computations:

Depreciation on *cost* ($500 × .20)	$100
Depreciation on *real* cost saving increment to asset ($25 × .20)	5
Depreciation on *fictional* cost saving increment to asset ($50 × .20)	10
Total depreciation for 19B ($575 × .20)	$115

Historical Cost Entries			*CRC Entries*		
6. To record realization of cost savings:					
No entry			Unrealized cost saving, real	5	
			Unrealized cost saving, fictional	10	
			Realized cost saving, real		5
			Realized cost saving, fictional		10

These amounts, like those in entry 5, are based on the asset increments entered in the accounts at entry 4.

Now we may proceed to the 19B CRC income statement and year-end balance sheet. Illustration 25–3 presents those financial statements.

Illustration 25–3

CORPORATION
Income Statement—CRC Basis
Year Ended December 31, 19B

Service revenue		$700
Expenses:		
Depreciation	$115	
Other	400	515
Current operating profit		185
Add cost savings:		
Realized—real	5	
Unrealized—real	20	25
Net income—CRC Basis		$210

CORPORATION
Balance Sheet—CRC Basis
December 31, 19B

Cash		$ 350
Accounts receivable		350
Fixed asset—cost		500
Unrealized cost, saving, real		25
Unrealized cost saving, fictional		50
Accumulated depreciation—cost		(200)
Unrealized cost saving, real		(5)
Unrealized cost saving, fictional		(10)
		$1,060
Liabilities		$ 400
Owners' Equity:		
Beginning, at cost	$400	
Realized cost saving, fictional	10	
Unrealized cost saving, fictional	40	
Beginning, CRC basis	450	
Add: Net income, CRC basis	210	
Ending, CRC basis		660
		$1,060

Illustration 25–3 portrays another desirable feature of the CRC model, namely that it is possible to match current costs against current revenues and *concurrently* present balance sheet accounts at current cost. The Lifo inventory method accomplishes the former but falls woefully short in terms of the latter objective of financial reporting.

True or false? Refer, if necessary, to illustrations 25–1, 25–2, and 25–3.

______ 1. The CRC financial statements present a more favorable image of the hypothetical Corporation than the historical cost financial statements.

______ 2. CRC accounting is really quite similar to general purchasing power accounting in terms of the accounts which are affected by the adjustments to the historical cost balances.

______ 3. The balance in the asset increment accounts (for cost savings) will always be unrealized.

______ 4. The reporting of real unrealized cost savings as an element of income represents a departure from the realization principle of the traditional historical cost accounting model.

Now check your responses by referring to Answer Frame 1[25], page 116.

Answer frame 1[25]

1. True *or* false. The answer depends, in general, on the relative importance accorded by the statement user to the results of (*a*) operating activities (i.e., current operating profit) and (*b*) buying and holding activities (i.e., cost savings). But, the CRC model separates the results of the two activities.
2. True. For most entities, the current replacement costs, or price-level adjusted costs, of fixed assets and inventories are more likely to differ from historical costs than for most other accounts.
3. True. By definition, assets are unexpired costs. Accordingly, the asset increment accounts pertain in a CRC context to *unrealized* elements of cost saving.
4. True. The rationale for so reporting real unrealized cost saving is that it represents economic betterment to the firm even though the asset to which it pertains has not yet been converted to revenue. And, consistent with the traditional reporting framework, economic betterments are reported on the income statement. Note, however, that cost savings are separated from operating activities.

If you missed any of the above questions, reread Frame 1[25] before proceeding. Then go on to Frame 2[25], below.

Frame 2[25]

Market Value Accounting

The theoretical value of any asset is the present value of the future cash flows the asset can be used to generate. Furthermore, market values (i.e., selling prices) in general tend to reflect these theoretical values. Therefore, the market value of an asset is a good first approximation of its discounted cash flows. Proponents of market value accounting hold that the most decision-relevant economic information about an asset, or about an entire entity, is its current market value. They hold that virtually all decisions pertaining to the item (or entity) implicitly consider its market value. They also hold that historical costs are sunk costs and as such are not relevant to current decision making.

Income in the pure form of the market value model is easy to compute because it is simply the difference in the market value of the entity measured at two points in time, adjusted for capital contributions, dividends, and other capital changes. Therefore, the market value method stands alone insofar as income is measured—in that the model does not utilize the matching principle. Furthermore, the market value method also differs from the other models in terms of recognizing income that has not been realized. Proponents of the model view this as a distinct advantage because it reduces the ability of firms to "manage" their earnings. To illustrate this point, assume that a firm had one asset, an investment portfolio of stocks, that it acquired for a cash outlay of $50,000 on June 30, 19B. On December 31, 19B, its next balance sheet date, the firm's portfolio was worth $55,000 and then six months later it was sold for $54,000. Market value accounting for this firm would dictate that it recognize $5,000 of income during 19B and a loss of $1,000 during 19C. Under the historical cost model, the firm's management could time the sale of the securities so as to report the profit (or loss) on the sale when they desired. In this case, they would report in 19C a $4,000 gain on the sale.

Critics of the method are quick to point out that market values are relevant data for specific assets such as inventories and investments which are expected to be converted to cash over the short term, but not so relevant for valuing such assets as plant and equipment, which are converted to cash by more complex processes. Critics note that these operating assets are not frequently sold prior to disposal and conclude on that basis that selling prices (especially those obtained from secondhand markets) do not often measure the usefulness of such assets to their owners. Market value proponents counter with the argument that all assets, except land, are in a perpetual state of liquidation, which suggests that market values are the more relevant data. And so the debate continues.

Few accountants are strongly opposed to certain versions of market value accounting on purely theoretical grounds. The most significant problems with the method concern its practical implementation. Much of the market value data is simply not available, and where it is available, some market value quotes do not agree with others—for a given item. This makes clear the problem inherent in any method based on *value,* namely that *value is* determined by a subjective process which is very difficult to model. There is little doubt that the degree of subjectivity involved in setting values that are *not* manifest in arm's-length transactions accounts for most of the criticism of market value accounting. In this regard, it is interesting that (unrealized) market values are accorded treatment in the historical cost framework, but only where the evidence thereof is generally quite objective. The applications, of course, are to inventories and investments, where the lower-of-cost-or-market rule presupposes that (objective) market values can be obtained. It is also worth noting that valuation of investment portfolios at market (whether above or below cost) is generally accepted for investment-related companies such as mutual funds.

Overview of CRC and Market Value Accounting

In 1976 the Securities and Exchange Commission (SEC) of the U.S. Treasury Department began requiring the largest corporations in the United States to disclose, in footnote form, the current cost of replacing inventories and productive capacity as well as cost of sales and depreciation, depletion, and amortization expense based on current replacement cost. This mandate thus accorded current value accounting a measure of acceptability that it had formerly possessed only in academic circles. The SEC stated publicly that it invited experimentation with different ways of measuring current replacement costs and that indeed it was not irreversibly committed to CRC accounting. The organized accounting profession was thereby offered a challenge to devise better ways of measuring the significant economic activities of business enterprises. The generally accepted accounting model of the next generation, perhaps of the next few years, will very likely be a hybrid of the features of all four models: historical cost, general purchasing power, current replacement cost, and market value. The features which comprise the model of the future must possess an appropriate blend of decision relevance, objectivity, and feasibility of application.

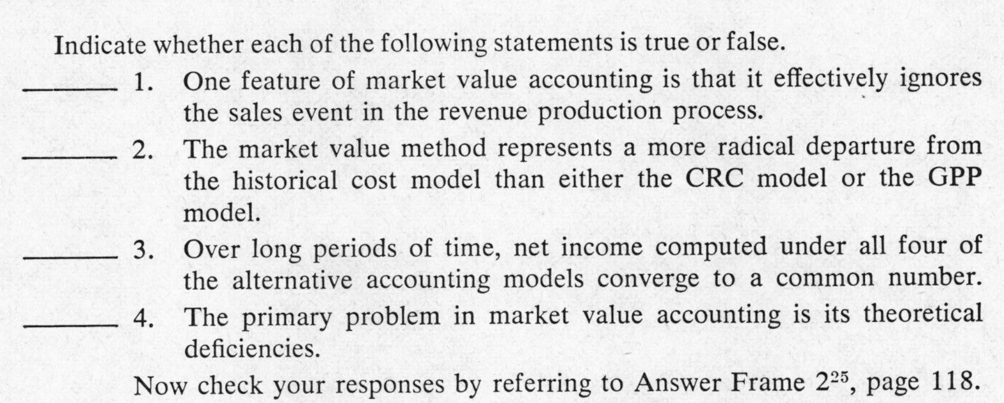

Indicate whether each of the following statements is true or false.

______ 1. One feature of market value accounting is that it effectively ignores the sales event in the revenue production process.

______ 2. The market value method represents a more radical departure from the historical cost model than either the CRC model or the GPP model.

______ 3. Over long periods of time, net income computed under all four of the alternative accounting models converge to a common number.

______ 4. The primary problem in market value accounting is its theoretical deficiencies.

Now check your responses by referring to Answer Frame 2^{25}, page 118.

Answer frame 2[25]

1. True. This is one theoretical objection raised to the pure form of the market value method. Many accountants who are favorably impressed with the decision relevance of current market values nevertheless view the completed sales transaction as being an important element in the earnings process.
2. True. This is seen in three related features of the market value method. One feature is the fact that the model ignores the matching principle. The second is that market values preempt costs as soon as the two differ for a given item. The third is that the market value method completely ignores the sales event for purposes of recognizing revenue. By contrast, the other three methods utilize matching, maintain cost in the accounts and/or represent adjustments to cost, and place a great deal of importance on the sales event, respectively.
3. False. The statement is likely to be true for historical cost, CRC, and market value methods. Aggregate net income, computed on a GPP basis, will probably not equal the other (common) net income because many entities' resources (i.e., assets and equities) will be unique and therefore may differ markedly from the items used to compute the general price-level index.
4. False. Market value accounting is sound theoretically. The primary problem is implementation (i.e., objective determination of market values).

If you missed any of the above, restudy Frame 2[25]. You have now completed this PLAID on intermediate accounting. Work Examination 6 on page 127 to further test your understanding.

Sample examination questions

Examination 4—chapters 15–18

The reader should note that while most of the examination questions are cast in the multiple choice format, the content of the questions could be covered in a variety of different ways. That is, the questions involve (*a*) theoretical concepts, (*b*) journal entries, (*c*) computations, (*d*) short answers and the like. Answers to the questions, along with explanations and computations, are given beginning on page 133.

1. Assuming the issuing company has only one class of stock, a transfer from retained earnings to capital stock equal to the market value of the shares issued is ordinarily a characteristic of—
   a. Either a stock dividend or a stock split.
   b. Neither a stock dividend nor a stock split.
   c. A stock split but not a stock dividend.
   d. A stock dividend but not a stock split.
2. Stock warrants outstanding should be classified as—
   a. Liabilities.
   b. Reductions of capital contributed in excess of par.
   c. Capital stock.
   d. Additions to contributed capital.
3. For a two-year period following a properly implemented quasi-reorganization, Bruno Corporation operated profitably and paid dividends equal to 20% of its net income each of the two years. How could one determine that the quasi-reorganization had occurred?
   a. Could *not* unless comparative balance sheets were presented.
   b. By the nature of the reserves in the stockholders' equity section.
   c. By the dating of retained earnings.
   d. By the conservative dividend policy.
4. Gordon Corporation has 50,000 shares of $10 par-value common stock authorized, issued, and outstanding. All 50,000 shares were issued at $12 per share. Retained earnings of the company are $60,000. If 1,000 shares of Gordon common stock were reacquired at $15 per share and the par-value method of accounting for treasury stock were used,
   a. Stockholders' equity would increase $15,000.
   b. Contributed capital in excess of par would decrease by at least $2,000.
   c. Retained earnings would decrease $5,000.
   d. Common stock would decrease $15,000.

5. Refer to the facts in Question 4 above. If the 1,000 shares that were reacquired were reissued at $11 per share and the cost method were used for recording the reacquisition,
   a. Book value per share of common would decrease.
   b. Retained earnings would decrease $11,000.
   c. Donated Surplus would be credited for $5,500.
   d. The Loss on Reissue of Treasury Stock would be debited.
6. The directors of Corel Corporation, whose $40 par-value common stock is currently selling at $50 per share, have decided to issue a stock dividend. The corporation has an authorization for 200,000 shares of common, has issued 110,000 shares of which 10,000 shares are now held as treasury stock, and desires to capitalize $400,000 of the Retained Earnings balance. To accomplish this, the percentage of stock dividend that the directors should declare is:
   a. 10.
   b. 8.
   c. 5.
   d. 20.
7. When a corporation issues preferred stock for land, the land should be recorded at:
   a. Total par value of the stock issued.
   b. Total book value of the stock issued.
   c. Fair market value of the land.
   d. Total liquidating value of the stock issued.
8. Compensation measured under a compensatory stock option plan should be reflected as:
   a. A charge against paid-in capital.
   b. A charge against retained earnings.
   c. A current liability.
   d. An income statement charge.
9. Gains on sales of treasury stock should be credited to:
   a. Additional paid-in capital.
   b. Capital stock.
   c. Retained earnings.
   d. Other income.
10. When a corporation declares a dividend to be paid in noncash property, the appropriate amount on which to base the dividend entries is:
   a. Carrying value of the assets to be distributed.
   b. Valuation of the assets set by the board of directors.
   c. Fair market value of the assets to be distributed.
   d. Par value of an equivalent amount of stock.

The following facts pertain to Questions 11 and 12.
Corporation H has the following capital structure:

Preferred stock, 6%, 10,000 shares authorized, issued, and outstanding, par $10	$100,000
Common stock, 20,000 shares authorized, 5,000 shares issued and outstanding, par $5	25,000

11. Preferred is noncumulative and nonparticipating. Dividends of $15,000 are declared. The allocation is:
   a. $10,000 to preferred and $5,000 to common.
   b. $6,000 to preferred and $9,000 to common.
   c. $5,000 to preferred and $10,000 to common.
   d. None of the above.

12. Preferred is cumulative and fully participating. Three years' preferred dividends are in arrears, and dividends of $28,000 are declared. The allocation is:
    a. $24,800 to preferred and $3,200 to common.
    b. $26,000 to preferred and $2,000 to common.
    c. $20,000 to preferred and $8,000 to common.
    d. None of the above.

13. Beame Corporation is developing its earnings per share (EPS) presentation at December 31, 19A. The records of the company provide the following information:

Liabilities:	
Convertible bonds payable, 7% (each $1,000 bond is convertible into 25 shares of common stock)	$200,000
Stockholders' Equity:	
Preferred stock, $10 par, 6% paid on dates when calendar quarters end, authorized 20,000 shares:	
Outstanding January 1, 19A, 3,000 shares	
Issued July 1, 19A, 2,000 shares	50,000
Contributed capital in excess of par, preferred stock	10,000
Common stock, nopar, authorized 100,000 shares:	
Outstanding January 1, 19A, 59,000 shares	
Issued 10,000 shares on April 1, 19A	360,000
Common stock warrants outstanding (for 4,000 shares of common stock)	16,000
Retained earnings	80,000
Income before extraordinary items	150,000
Extraordinary loss (net of tax)	(20,000)
Net Income	130,000

Other data:

1. Stock warrants—option price $4 per share; average market price of the common stock during 19A, $5.
2. Convertible bonds—issue price, 115; prime interest rate at date of issuance was 8%.
3. Average income tax rate of 45%.

Required:

Prepare the required EPS presentation for 19A.

14. On January 1, Ralph Corporation paid $8,000 cash for a 40% interest in Dudley Joe Corporation. At the time, the two corporations' balance sheets were as follows:

	Ralph Corp.	*Dudley Joe Corp.*
Cash	$ 10,000	$ 6,000
Receivables	4,000	3,000
Inventory	8,000	4,000
Fixed assets (net)	16,000	12,000
Current liabilities	(3,000)	(4,000)
Long-term debt	(10,000)	(6,000)
Common stock	(10,000)	(10,000)
Additional paid-in capital	(10,000)	(4,000)
Retained earnings	(5.000)	(1,000)
	–0–	–0–

On the date Ralph Corporation made the investment, Dudley Joe Corporation's inventories were valued at $5,000, and its fixed assets were valued at $14,000. The market values of all other items equaled book value.

During the following year, Dudley Joe Corporation earned $4,000 ordinary income and incurred a nonrecurring loss of $2,000. Dudley Joe Corporation declared a cash dividend of $1,500 on December 31 (its books close at the same date). *All* long-term assets are expected to have economic lives of ten years.

Required:

Make all entries pertinent to its investment in Dudley Joe Corporation on Ralph Corporation's books for the year ended December 31.

Now turn to page 133 to check your answers.

Sample examination questions

Examination 5—chapters 19–21

Answers are given, along with explanations and computations where needed, beginning on page 136.

1. On January 1, 19A, an investor purchased a one-year bond with a maturity value of $10,000. The nominal interest rate was 7%, paid semiannually. If the investor purchased the bonds to yield 8% to maturity, the amount paid would be:
   a. $9,893.
   b. $9,906.
   c. $9,550.
   d. $9,814.
2. On January 1, 19A, an investor paid $9,700 for bonds, face value of $10,000. The nominal interest rate on the bonds was 9%, and the market rate of interest at the time of the purchase was 10%. Interest is paid on the bonds each December 31. If the market interest rate changed during 19B to 9%, how much interest revenue would the investor earn on the bonds during 19B?
   a. $977.
   b. $900.
   c. $970.
   d. $1,000.
3. On September 30, 1977, you acquired $10,000 of 6%, 20-year bonds that mature on August 1, 1989. The bonds pay interest on February 1 and August 1. Premium or discount on bonds is amortized by the straight-line method. On December 31, 1977, you made the following adjusting entry relative to the bond investment:

Interest receivable	250	
Investment in 6% bonds	45	
Interest revenue		295

   The purchase price of the bond excluding accrued interest was:
   a. $7,870.
   b. $7,750.
   c. $7,900.
   d. None of the above.

4. Generally accepted accounting principles, namely *APB Opinion No. 26* plus FASB *Statement No. 4,* require that gains or losses on refunding bonds payable be:
   a. Charged to Retained Earnings as an adjustment of prior years' net incomes.
   b. Recognized in the current year income statement as an extraordinary item of gain or loss on refunding.
   c. Amortized over the remaining life of the old *refunded* issue as an adjustment of interest expense on the old issue.
   d. Amortized over the life of the new *refunding* issue on the theory that the new bonds are merely an extension of the old bonds.

5. Convertible bonds typically bear an interest rate that is:
   a. Lower than the rate on comparable nonconvertible bonds.
   b. Higher than the rate on comparable nonconvertible bonds.
   c. Generally the same as the rate on comparable nonconvertible bonds.
   d. Not related in any systematic way to the rate on comparable nonconvertible bonds.

6. Changes in accounting principles are, with a few exceptions, given—
   a. Retroactive effect.
   b. Current effect.
   c. Prospective effect.
   d. Current and pro forma effect.

7. Firm L paid $4,000 for a truck and depreciated it for two years on the straight-line method (four-year useful life and $500 estimated residual value). Beginning with Year 3 the firm changed to SYD depreciation and retained the four-year life and $500 estimate of residual value.
   The comparative income statements of Firm L for Years 2 and 3 will report:
   a. Depreciation Expense of $875 for Year 2, Depreciation Expense of $875 for Year 3, and a Prior Period Adjustment of $1,750.
   b. Depreciation Expense of $875 for Year 2, Depreciation Expense of $700 for Year 3, and a Prior Period Adjustment of $700.
   c. Depreciation Expense of $875 for Year 2, Depreciation Expense of $700 for Year 3, and a catch-up adjustment of $700.
   d. Depreciation Expense of $1,050 for Year 2, Depreciation Expense of $700 for Year 3, and a catch-up adjustment of $1,400.

The following facts pertain to Questions 8 and 9:

Firm N has been depreciating a building (cost, $100,000; residual value, $10,000) over 30 years. At the end of 13 years, Firm N decides that the building will remain in service for a total of 40 years. It revises its depreciation computations accordingly, leaving all other factors unchanged.

8. The catch-up adjustment of Firm N during the year of the change will amount to:
   a. $39,000.
   b. $0.
   c. $29,250.
   d. $10,000.

9. Firm N's comparative income statements will report Depreciation Expense for the change year and the preceding year, respectively, of—
   a. $3,000 and $3,000.
   b. $3,000 and $2,250.
   c. $2,250 and $2,250.
   d. None of the above.

10. The bookkeeper of Latsch Company, which has an accounting year ending December 31, made the following errors:

    1. A $1,000 collection from a customer was received on December 29, 19A, but not recorded until the date of its deposit in the bank, January 4, 19B.
    2. A supplier's $1,600 invoice for inventory items received in December 19A was not recorded until January 19B. (Inventories at December 31, 19A, and 19B were correctly stated based on physical count.)
    3. Depreciation for 19A was understated by $900.
    4. In September 19A, a $200 invoice for office supplies was charged to the Utilities Expense account. Office supplies are expensed as purchased.
    5. December 31, 19A, sales on account of $3,000 were recorded in January 19B.

    Assume that no other errors have occurred and that no correcting entries have been made. *Ignore income taxes.* Net income for 19A was:
    a. Understated by $500.
    b. Understated by $2,100.
    c. Overstated by $2,500.
    d. Neither understated nor overstated.
    e. None of the above.

11. Assume the same facts as in Question 10. Working capital at December 31, 19A, was:
    a. Understated by $3,000.
    b. Understated by $500.
    c. Understated by $1,400.
    d. Neither understated nor overstated.
    e. None of the above.

12. On April 15, 19D, a fire destroyed the entire merchandise inventory of J. Anderson's retail store. The following data are available:

Sales, January 1 through April 15	$72,000
Inventory, January 1	10,000
Purchases, January 1 through April 15 . .	70,000
Markup on cost	20%

    The amount of the loss is estimated to be:
    a. $24,000.
    b. $20,000.
    c. $22,400.
    d. $8,000.

Questions 13–15 pertain to the statement of changes in financial position (SCFP) on the working capital basis.

13. The SCFP is:
    a. A supplement to the primary financial statements.
    b. Essentially equivalent to footnote disclosure.
    c. A primary financial statement.
    d. A secondary financial statement.

14. The SCFP presents—
    a. Financing activities.
    b. Investing activities.
    c. Financing and investing activities.
    d. Financing and investing activities, plus reasons for changes in working capital.

15. It takes Firm A exactly one year to use up existing current assets. Firm A recognized $100,000 of income tax expense during the year of which $24,000 related to installment sales that will be collected evenly over the next two years. The balance of $76,000 related to ordinary sales for which the income tax liability will be paid currently. Relative to the above, Firm A will report on its current year SCFP:
    a. Expense of $24,000 added back to net income before extraordinary items.
    b. Expense of $12,000 added back to net income before extraordinary items.
    c. Income tax expense of $76,000.
    d. None of the above.

Now turn to page 136 to check your answers.

Sample examination questions

Examination 6—chapters 22–25

Answers are given, along with explanations and computations where needed, beginning on page 139.

1. If a pension plan is funded over a period that exceeds the period over which the related expense is recognized, the employer firm will report—
   a. Pension liability.
   b. Prepaid pension expense.
   c. Actuarial gains or losses.
   d. Past service cost.
2. Generally accepted accounting principles (i.e., *APB Opinion No. 8*) require that past service cost be recognized:
   a. As a prior period adjustment to Retained Earnings.
   b. In the period when the pension plan is begun.
   c. Over a specified number of future periods.
   d. Over a number of future periods that fall within a specified range.
3. For purposes of distinguishing between distinctly different ways of accounting for lessees' leases, the categories of leases are:
   a. Financing leases and capital leases.
   b. Leveraged leases and capital leases.
   c. Operating leases and capital leases.
   d. Operating leases, sales-type leases, and financing leases.
   e. None of the above.

The following facts pertain to Questions 4 and 5.

A noncancelable lease agreement specifies the following:
   a. Title retained by lessor.
   b. Lessor's cost of the asset: $25,000.
   c. Lease term: four years.
   d. Estimated life of the leased asset: six years.
   e. Estimated residual value of the leased asset at end of six years: $7,000.
   f. Economically realistic depreciation method: Double-declining balance.
   g. Lessee can purchase leased asset after three years' use for $7,500.
   h. Lessor's cost uncertainties: None.

i. Lessee's marginal borrowing rate: 8%.
j. Bank prime interest rate: 8%.
k. Annual lease rental due on January 1 of each of four years (rounded to nearest dollar), $8,387.
l. Investment tax credit of 10% retained by lessor.
m. Fair market value of leased asset to lessor at inception of lease, $30,000.
n. Lessee makes no guarantee regarding residual value of the leased asset.

4. Lessee's entry to record the initial transaction under the above lease would be:

		Debit	Credit
a.	Leased property	30,000	
	Deferred lease expense	3,548	
	Cash		8,387
	Lease liability		25,161
b.	Leased property	27,779	
	Cash		8,387
	Lease liability		19,392
c.	Lease expense	8,387	
	Cash		8,387
d.	Leased property	33,548	
	Cash		8,387
	Lease liability		25,161

5. Lessor's entry to record the initial transaction under the above lease would be:

		Debit	Credit
a.	Gross investment in sales-type lease	33,548	
	Asset		25,000
	Unearned lease revenue		8,548
b.	Gross investment in sales-type lease	25,161	
	Cash	8,387	
	Asset		25,000
	Unearned lease revenue		8,548
c.	Gross investment in direct financing lease	25,161	
	Cash	8,387	
	Asset		27,779
	Unearned lease revenue		5,769
d.	Gross investment in sales-type lease	25,161	
	Cash	8,387	
	Sales revenue		30,000
	Unearned lease revenue		3,548
e.	Cash	8,387	
	Unearned lease revenue		8,387

6. If current assets equal $20,000, current liabilities equal $10,000, prepaid expenses and merchandise inventory equal $2,000 and $4,000, respectively, the quick ratio must be:
a. 1.4 to 1.
b. 1.6 to 1.
c. 1.8 to 1.
d. 2.0 to 1.

7. Firm H has the following equities at book value, which are constant during 19B:

Current liabilities	$10,000
Long-term debt, all at 8%	30,000
Preferred stockholders' equity, 10%	5,000
Common stockholders' equity	30,000

During 19B, Firm H earns net income of $6,000 and pays $300 cash dividends on preferred stock and $1,000 cash dividends on common stock. Firm H is in the 35% income tax bracket for 19B.

The return on Firm H's common stockholders' equity is:

a. 20.00%.
b. 15.67%.
c. 19.00%.
d. 18.33%.
e. None of the above.

8. It is virtually impossible for the merchandise turnover of a profit-oriented company to be:
   a. Too high.
   b. Too low.
   c. About right.
   d. Relatively constant from period to period.
   e. None of the above.

Hereafter abbreviate general purchasing power financial statements as "GPP F/S."

9. GPP F/S are likely to be *most* useful when—
   a. Prices rise dramatically.
   b. Prices stay relatively constant.
   c. Prices decline dramatically.
   d. Prices change dramatically.

10. On which of the following items does a company not recognize a GPP gain or loss, in preparing GPP F/S?
    a. Accounts receivable.
    b. Merchandise inventory.
    c. Notes receivable, long term.
    d. Bonds payable.
    e. Cash dividends payable.

Questions 11 and 12 utilize the following data:

Date	*Price Index Value*
12/31/19A	165
6/30/19B	175
12/31/19B	186
6/30/19C	194
9/30/19C	198
10/1/19C	198
12/31/19C	201
1/1/19D	201
3/31/19D	203
6/30/19D	206
9/30/19D	210
12/31/19D	212

11. On June 30, 19B, O, Inc., had as its only asset $5,000 in cash. On the same day, O, Inc., spent the cash to acquire a machine for $5,000. The machine is being depreciated over five years on the straight-line method with an estimated residual value of $500 (stated in June 30, 19B dollars). On September 30, 19D, O, Inc., purchased merchandise inventory on account for $1,000. These are the only transactions O, Inc., entered into from June 30, 19B, until January 1, 19E. At December

31, 19D, O, Inc., will report total assets, adjusted for GPP and stated in terms of December 31, 19D, dollars, of:

a. $4,341.
b. $6,913.
c. $7,067.
d. $6,475.

12. N Company made sales of $4,000 evenly during the fiscal year ended September 30, 19D. Also, during 19D, N Company received four quarterly interest revenue amounts the company earned on a bond investment that it purchased on January 1, 19D, at par. The quarterly interest checks of $300 each were collected on January 31, April 30, July 31, and October 31. N Company had no transactions during 19D other than those listed. For the year ended September 30, 19D, N Company will report GPP-adjusted total revenue of:
a. $4,044.
b. $5,048.
c. $4,346.
d. $6,037.
e. None of the above.

Questions 13–15 utilize the following data:

Firm A acquired a fixed asset on 1/1/19A for $1,000 when the price index stood at 100. At the end of the period (December 31, 19A), the price index was at 110, and the current replacement cost of the fixed asset was $1,250.

13. If the fixed asset was Firm A's only asset, had no residual value, and was being depreciated over five years on the straight-line method, Firm A's total depreciation expense for 19A, on a current replacement cost basis, is:
a. $220.
b. $200.
c. $205.
d. $250.

14. Refer to the facts pertaining to Question 13. Firm A will report on its current replacement cost balance sheet as of December 31, 19A, fictional realized cost savings and fictional realizable cost savings of:
a. $50 and $200, respectively.
b. $30 and $120, respectively.
c. $20 and $80, respectively.
d. None of the above.

15. If firm A had service revenues during 19A of $300, it would report current operating profit on a current replacement cost basis of:
a. $250.
b. $300.
c. $50.
d. $0.

16. As between the three alternative accounting models, historical cost, GPP, and current replacement cost, which will produce the highest net income during a period of rising prices for a company with current assets equal to current liabilities and fixed assets exceeding long-term debt?
a. Historical cost.
b. GPP.

c. Current replacement cost.
d. All three are the same.
e. Cannot be determined from the information given.

Now turn to page 139 to check your answers.

Answers to sample examination questions

Examination 4—chapters 15–18

1. *d.*
2. *d.*
3. *c.*
4 *b.* Explanation: Contributed capital prior to purchase of treasury stock:

Common Stock		Contributed Capital in Excess of Par, Common		Retained Earnings	
	500,000		100,000		60,000

Entry to record purchase of treasury stock:

Treasury stock—common	10,000	
Contributed capital in excess of par—common	2,000	
Retained earnings	3,000	
Cash		15,000

Resulting balances in the accounts after purchase:

Common Stock		Contributed Capital in Excess of Par, Common		Retained Earnings		Treasury Stock—Common	
	500,000	2,000	100 000	3,000	60.000	10,000	
			98,000		57,000		

Conclusion is that contributed capital in excess of par is reduced by $2,000. If there had been another contributed capital account associated with the common, that additional account could have been debited for some or all of the $3,000, in which case the reduction in contributed capital in excess of par would have exceeded $2,000.

5. *a.* Explanation: Entry under cost method to record purchase of treasury stock:

Treasury stock—common	15,000	
Cash		15,000

Entry to record resale for $11,000:

Cash	11,000	
Contributed capital in excess of par, common	2,000	
Retained earnings	2,000	
Treasury stock—common		15,000

Conclusion is that debits to contributed capital in excess of par and retained earnings reduce book value per share of common (book value equals common equity divided by number of common shares outstanding).

6. *b.* Explanation: Corel desires to capitalize $400,000, which is related to some number of shares. The per share amount is either par value or current market value, depending on whether the dividend is "large" or "small," respectively. Therefore, try par value of $40 per share.

   $400,000/$40 = 10,000 shares/100,000 shares = 10%, which is a "small" stock dividend. Par value is not used for "small" stock dividends.

   Therefore, try current value of $50.

   $400,000/$50 = 8,000 shares/100,000 shares = 8%, "small." This is consistent.

7. *c.*
8. *d.*
9. *a.*
10. *c.*
11. *b.*
12. *b.* Explanation:

	Preferred	*Common*
Arrearage to preferred, 6% × $100,000 × 3	$18,000	
Current year dividend to preferred, 6% × $100,000	6,000	
Pro rata current year dividend to common, 6% × $25,000 . .		$1,500
Participation based on relative par values:		
Preferred: $28,000 − ($18,000 + $6,000 + $1,500) =		
$2,500 × ($100,000/$125,000)	2,000	
Common: $2,500 × ($25,000/$125,000)		500
Total of $28,000	$26.000	$2,000

13.

Primary EPS:

Net income before extraordinary items $\dfrac{\$150{,}000 - \$2{,}400^{*}}{(59{,}000 \times 1/4) + (69{,}000 \times 3/4) + 800^{\dagger}} = \$2.193$

Extraordinary loss (net of tax) $\dfrac{\$20{,}000}{67{,}300} =$ (.297)

Net income $\dfrac{\$127{,}600}{67{,}300} =$ $1.896

Fully diluted EPS:

Net income before extraordinary items $\dfrac{\$147{,}600 + \$7{,}700^{\ddagger}}{67{,}300 + 5{,}000^{\ddagger}} =$ $2.148

Extraordinary loss (net of tax) $\dfrac{\$20{,}000}{72{,}300} =$ (.277)

Net income $\dfrac{\$135{,}300}{72{,}300} =$ $1.871

Computations:

* Preferred dividends for 19A:

(3,000 × $10) × 6% × 1/2 year =	$ 900
(5,000 × $10) × 6% × 1/2 year =	1,500
	$2,400

† Dilution from stock warrants:
4,000 × $4 = $16,000/$5 = 3,200 shares
4,000 shares − 3,200 shares = 800 shares dilution.

Prime rate test for possible classification of convertible bonds as common stock equivalents (CSEs):

$$\frac{.07 \text{ (nominal interest rate)}}{1.15 \text{ (issue price of bonds)}} = 6.09\% \text{ true yield rate on bonds}$$

Prime interest rate: $.08 \times 2/3 = 5.33\%$

Yield rate exceeds 2/3 prime rate. Therefore, convertible bonds are *not* CSEs and hence are not used to compute primary EPS.

‡ *Convertible bonds antidilutive?:*

Aftertax interest: .07 ($200,000) (1.00 − .45) = $7,700
Number of shares into which bonds are convertible: 200 × 25 = 5,000

$7,700/5,000 shares = $1.54. The quotient of $1.54 is less than primary EPS before extraordinary items ($2.193); therefore the convertible bonds are dilutive and as such are used to compute fully diluted EPS.

14. *a.* At date of acquisition:

Long-term investment in stock of DJ Corporation	8,000	
Cash		8,000

At year-end:

b. To recognize Ralph's proportionate share of Dudley Joe's operating results:

Long-term investment in stock of DJ Corporation	800	
Investment loss—nonrecurring ($2,000 × .40)	800	
Investment revenue—ordinary ($4,000 × .40)		1,600

c. To record excess depreciation on cost of Dudley Joe's depreciable assets:

Investment revenue—ordinary [($14,000 − $12,000)/10].40	80	
Long-term investment in DJ Corporation		80

d. To amortize goodwill implicit in acquisition price:

Investment revenue—ordinary	80	
Long-term investment in DJ Corporation		80

Computations:

Acquisition price of DJ Corporation			$8,000
Fair market value at acquisition date of identifiable net assets of DJ Corporation:			
DJ owners' equity at book value		$15,000	
Add: Market value increments to—			
Inventory	1,000		
Fixed assets	2,000	3,000	
		18,000	
Ralph's ownership percentage		× .40	
Fair market value of Ralph's proportionate share of DJ Corporation's identifiable net assets			7,200
Difference—goodwill			800
Estimated useful life in years			÷ 10
Annual amount of goodwill amortization			$ 80

e. To record DJ Corporation's dividend declaration:

Dividend receivable ($1,500 × .40)	600	
Long-term investment in DJ Corporation		600

Answers to sample examination questions

Examination 5—chapters 19–21

1. *b.* Computations:

$$V = \$10{,}000 \times p_{\substack{n=2 \\ i=4\%}} + \$350 \times P_{\substack{n=2 \\ i=4\%}}$$
$$= (\$10{,}000 \times .924556) + (\$350 \times 1.8861) = \underline{\underline{\$9{,}905.69}}$$

2. *a.* Explanation: It is convenient to prepare a present value amortization table to solve this problem. It should also be noted that the fact that the market interest rate changes during 19B has no effect on the *purchaser's* yield rate on the bond investment. Also, use of straight-line amortization would be difficult because the period to maturity is not given.

Date	*Cash Receipts of Interest*	*Interest Income*	*Amortization of Discount*	*Investment Carrying Value*
1/1/19A				$9,700
12/31/19A	$900[a]	$970[b]	$70[c]	9,770[d]
12/31/19B		977		

[a] $900 = .09 × $10,000
[b] $970 = .10 × $9,700
[c] $70 = $970 − $900
[d] $9,770 = $9,700 + $70

3. *a.* Explanation: This problem requires you to work backwards from the end-of-period adjusting entry to the entry to record acquisition of the bond investment. Therefore, it is necessary to identify each item in the adjusting entry with its related period of time. The results will be (*a*) the amount of interest per period and (*b*) the amount of discount amortization per period. These amounts may then be used to produce the acquisition entry.

Interest receivable of $250 relates to August 1–December 31, a five-month period, or cash interest of $50 per month. This is consistent with (6% × $10,000)/12 months = $50 per month.

Discount amortization of $45 relates to September 30–December 31, a three-month period, or $15 per month. The bonds had a life of 142 months from acquisition to maturity on August 1, 1989. Therefore, the total discount (from par) at date of acquisition was 142 × $15 = $2,130, which implies a purchase price of $10,000 − $2,130 = $7,870, excluding accrued interest.

At acquisition date (9/30/77), interest had accrued for two months since the last interest date on 8/1/77. Thus, the accrued interest paid at acquisition was 2 × $50 = $100.

Based on the above, the acquisition entry must have been:

Investment in 6% bonds	7,870	
Interest revenue	100	
Cash		7,970

4. *b.*
5. *a.*
6. *d.*
7. *c.* Computations:

	Straight Line	*SYD*
\$3,500/4 = \$875 for Year 1	\$ 875	
= \$875 for Year 2	875	
\$3,500 × [4/(4 + 3 + 2 + 1)] = \$1,400 for Year 1 . . .		\$1,400
\$3,500 × 3/10 = \$1,050 for Year 2		1,050
Total depreciation for Years 1 and 2	\$1,750	\$2,450

Catch-up adjustment is \$700 difference between straight-line depreciation recorded (\$1,750) and SYD depreciation (\$2,450) that would have been recorded if SYD had been used in Years 1 and 2. This catch-up adjustment is reflected on the income statement of Year 3, the year of the accounting change.

The Year 3 income statement also reports SYD depreciation of \$700 (\$3,500 × 2/10). The comparative Year 2 income statement reports straight-line depreciation of \$875 that was actually recorded in Year 2. The Year 2 income statement is *not* restated to the new basis.

8. *b.* Explanation: There is no catch-up adjustment for changes in accounting estimates.
9. *d.* Computations:

(100,000 − \$10,000)/30 = \$3,000 per year × 13 = \$39,000.

Book value at end of 13 years is \$61,000 (\$100,000 − \$39,000). Of this \$61,000, only \$51,000 is depreciable over 27 remaining years. Therefore, annual straight-line depreciation for the change year is \$1,889 (\$51,000/27). Depreciation expense for the preceding year would be reported at \$3,000.

10. *a.* Computations (Let ↑ symbolize overstatement and ↓ understatement):

1. \$ 0
2. ↑ 1,600
3. ↑ 900
4. 0
5. ↓ 3,000

↓\$ 500

11. *c.* Computations (Let ↑ symbolize overstatement and ↓ understatement):

1. \$ 0
2. ↑ 1,600
3. 0
4. 0
5. ↓ 3,000

↓\$1,400

12. *b.* Explanation: This problem uses the gross profit method of estimating ending inventory. The solution also utilizes the cost of goods sold model, that is, Beginning inventory + Purchases − Ending inventory = Cost of goods sold. In this problem, we know beginning inventory (\$10,000) and purchases (\$70,000). We can also compute cost of goods sold from sales and the markup on cost.

Sales = (1 + markup on cost) × cost of goods sold
\$72,000 = 1.20 × cost of goods sold
\$60,000 = cost of goods sold

Now we may solve for the loss (i.e., ending inventory):

Beginning inventory . . .	$10,000
+ Purchases	+70,000
− Ending inventory	− X
= Cost of goods sold	$60,000

X = $20,000

13. *c.*

14. *d.*

15. *b.* Explanation: Entry to record income taxes is:

Income tax expense	100,000	
Income tax payable		76,000
Deferred income tax—current		12,000
Deferred income tax—long term		12,000

The entry recorded a total reduction in net income of $100,000, whereas only $88,000 pertained to current liabilities (i.e., reductions in net working capital). As a result, $12,000 should be added back to net income before extraordinary items.

Answers to sample examination questions

Examination 6—chapters 22–25

1. *a.*
2. *d.*
3. *c.*
4. *a.* Explanation: First, lease must be classified as either *capital* or *operating* to the lessee. This particular lease agreement constitutes a *capital* lease to the lessee because (*a*) the lease contains a bargain purchase option and (*b*) the present value of the minimum lease payments exceeds 90% of the excess of the fair market value of the leased asset over the tax credit retained by the lessor. However, satisfaction of either condition (*a*) *or* (*b*) would be sufficient to classify the lease as *capital* to the lessee.

Proofs: *a.* To show the bargin purchase option, it is necessary to compare book value of the leased asset to the option price of the leased asset, both at the option date (which is at the end of three years). Thus, it is necessary to depreciate the asset for three years on the double-declining-balance depreciation method. Depreciation is:

($30,000 − $7,000) × (2 × 1/6) =	$ 7,667	for Year 1
($23,000 − $7,667) × (2 × 1/6) =	5,111	for Year 2
[$23,000 − ($7,667 + $5,111)] × (2 × 1/6) =	3,407	for Year 3
	$16,185	

Thus, the book value of the leased asset would be $13,815 ($30,000 − $16,185), and this makes it appear that the option price of $7,500 is indeed a *bargain* price.

b. To show satisfaction of the other condition, it is necessary to compute the present value of the four minimum lease payments of $8,387 each. Then this is compared to 90% of the excess of $30,000 fair market value over the 10% tax credit of $2,500 (computed on lessor's cost of $25,000).

Present value of minimum lease payments (V):

$$V = \$8,387 \times 3.577 \left(P_{\substack{n=4 \\ i=8\%}} \times 1.08 \right)$$

$V = \$30,000.$

Comparison*:

$\$30,000 > .90(\$30,000 - \$2,500).$

$\$30,000 > \$24,750.$

* Note that this comparison appears trivial in this problem. However, in cases in which the fair value of the leased asset exceeds the present value of the minimum lease payments, the comparison will not be trivial.

Now that the lease is classified as *capital,* the lessee may proceed directly to the entry of the leased asset in the accounts. The entry is:

Leased property ($8,387 × 3.577)	30,000	
Deferred lease expense	3,548	
Cash		8,387
Lease liability (3 × $8,387)		25,161

The debit of $3,548 to Deferred Lease Expense represents lease expense (interest) to be recognized over the four-year life of the lease. It is computed as follows:

Total minimum lease payments (4 × $8,387) . . .	$33,548
Present value of lease payments (*V* above) . . .	30,000
Deferred lease expense	$ 3,548

5. *d.* Explanation: The solution to Question 5 proceeds in a fashion similar to that of Question 4, and it also uses the same computations. Here the *lessor* must first classify his lease as a prelude to accounting for it. Lessor's lease turns out to be *sales type* because (*a*) lease is *capital* type to lessee *and* (*b*) lessor's marginal borrowing rate of 8% (same as prime rate) suggests lessee's creditworthiness *and* (*c*) lessor has no material cost uncertainties *and* (*d*) fair value of the leased asset ($30,000) exceeds lessor's carrying value of $25,000. Therefore, lessor's entry is:

Gross investment in sales-type lease (3 × $8,387)	25,161	
Cash	8,387	
Sales ($8,387 × 3.577)		30,000
Unearned lease revenue ($33,548 − $30,000 as above)		3,548

6. *a.* Explanation: Quick ratio = Quick assets/Current liabilities. Quick assets = cash, short-term investments, and current receivables. Therefore, inventories and prepaid expenses are excluded from the current assets to derive the quick assets. So, in this problem, quick assets equal $14,000 ($20,000 − $4,000 − $2,000) and current liabilities equal $10,000 (as given). Consequently, the quick ratio must be 1.4 to 1 ($14,000/$10,000).

7. *d.* Computation:

$$\frac{\text{Net income} - \text{Preferred dividends (whether or not declared)*}}{\text{Average common stockholders' equity}}$$

$$= \frac{\$6{,}000 - (.10 \times \$5{,}000)}{\$30{,}000} = \frac{\$\ 5{,}500}{\$30{,}000} = 18.33\%$$

* Recall that most states construe preferred stock to be cumulative in the absence of a statement to the contrary.

8. *e.* Explanation: Item A may appear at first to be an acceptable answer. However, it is possible for a merchandise turnover rate to be high. To see this, consider a company that has trouble obtaining its merchandise from its vendors. This company may be selling more merchandise than it has to sell, resulting in slow deliveries to its customers. Although not generally as bad as too low a turnover rate, too high a turnover rate can nevertheless present significant problems to the company organized for profit.

9. *d.* (*d*) is a better answer than either (*a*) or (*c*) because it includes both (*a*) and (*c*).

10. *b.* Explanation: Merchandise inventory is classified as nonmonetary. GPP gains or losses are recognized on monetary items, not on nonmonetary items such as inventory.

11. *a.* Computations:

Machine—cost ($5,000 × 212/175)	=	$6,057
—accumulated depreciation [($5,000 − $500)/5 = $900 × 2½ × 212/175]	=	(2,726)
Book value, stated in 12/31/19D dollars		$3,331
Inventory ($1,000 × 212/210)	=	1,010
Total assets at 12/31/19D, stated in 12/31/19D dollars		$4,341

12. *b.* Computations:

$$\text{Sales revenue } \$4{,}000 \times \frac{210}{(198 + 201 + 203 + 206 + 210)/5} = \quad \$4{,}126$$

Interest revenue (assumed to be earned evenly over the year):

$$\$100 \text{ per month} \times 9 \text{ months} \times \frac{210}{(201 + 203 + 206 + 210)/4} = \quad \underline{922}$$

Total revenue for fiscal 19D, stated in 9/30/19D dollars $\underline{\underline{\$5{,}048}}$

13. *d.* Computation: $1,250/5 = $250.
14. *c.* Explanation and computations: *Fictional* cost savings reflect the excess of replacement cost over historical cost, that is attributable solely to a rise in the general level of prices. On a separate dimension, *realized* cost savings are cost savings on assets that have been expensed (i.e., converted into revenue), and *realizable* cost savings are cost savings on remaining (i.e., undepreciated) assets. Therefore,

   Fictional cost savings:

$$\$1{,}000 \times 110/100 = \$1{,}100 - \$1{,}000 = \$100.$$

   Fictional realized cost savings:

$$\frac{\text{Depreciated cost of fixed asset}}{\text{Total cost of asset}} = \frac{\$\ 250}{\$1{,}250} \times \$100 = \$20.$$

   Fictional realizable cost savings:

$$\frac{\text{Book value of fixed asset}}{\text{Total cost of asset}} = \frac{\$1{,}000}{\$1{,}250} \times \$100 = \$80.$$

15. *c.* Explanation: Current operating profit = Revenue − Expenses stated in terms of current replacement costs. $300 − $250 = $50.
16. *e.* Explanation: The answer cannot be determined from the information given because:
    a. The comparison between historical cost and GPP requires knowledge of whether assets and liabilities are monetary or nonmonetary. Knowledge of whether they are current or long-term does not provide this information.
    b. The comparison of historical cost and current replacement cost requires knowledge of the current replacement cost of the firm's *specific assets*. This is not given.
    c. The comparison of GPP and current replacement cost cannot be made for reasons given in explanations (*a*) and (*b*) above.

INDEX

* Volume 2.

* Volume 2.

* Volume 2.